WOMEN ENTREPRENEUR

K. K. Singh

Gaurav Book Centre Pvt. Ltd.
New Delhi

Publisher
Gaurav Book Centre Pvt. Ltd.
4832/24,Prahlad Lane,S-207 Ansari, Road,
Daryaganj, Delhi-110002 Ph.: 43570976, 23278261
Email: gauravbookcentre@gmail.com

Edition: 2026

ISBN : 978-93-83316-07-6

Laser Typesetting
JEE-VEE Graphics Delhi

Price : 925.00

Printed by
Vikas Computers

PREFACE

This book has been designed to meet the requirements of All Ladies and Gents, NGOs who are dealing with all types of Entrepreneurship, Social Worker, Women Development Institutions and Academies and students studying at schools and colleges, the boys appearing at IAS opting Sociology as main subject and other social scientists who are doing a great deal for Women Entrepreneurship. It would be helpful for all who are dealing with Entrepreneurship. It will help in guiding the Indian Women towards making right effort for right functionality.

The present book is a novel attempt to cover a wide range of the problems of Personality Development in the segment of Development of Personality among the people of all kinds of personalities in the human beings of the world. This book faces very busy ideological preparedness in my life. It is in the context of managerial work that we have studied this aspect of English literature, but in this book it has by no means limited to that context. Busy idleness is a disease that affects everybody and pervades every aspect of life. Active non-action is the word that I would like to explain here.

In our professional life, we always face problems in the shape of daily problem solving activities. Problems require a big picture perspective—which means reflection, systematic planning, creative thinking and time. Operational activities squeeze important problems out. Daily routines, superficial behavior, poorly prioritized unfocused tasks leech managers` capacities- making unproductive business.

The problem is not a lack of knowledge or resources. The real problem is that they simply do not do those things. They spend their time spinning their wheels, attending meetings and responding to every little query and problem.

Management is "the art of getting things done." Managers must act themselves and mobilize collective action on the part of others. The gap between knowledge and action, stretches wide and few managers seem able to cross it. The kind of behavior that exhibited active non-action as it is called pervasive corporate "knowing-doing gap." Managers always complain about the problem of active non-action but have not fully understood the underlying dynamics.

When driven by deep personal commitment to the goal that cuts out distractions and overcomes difficulties. The purposeful action is not a quick shuffle or mere flirtation with ideas. It is action taking to produce certain results with undivided resolve. Although external issues in an organization can make this kind of action taking difficulties.

We are deeply indebted to all the Websites and Academicians, Researchers, HR professionals and all Managers who participated directly or indirectly in authoring this book, giving us generously not only their time but also their knowledge and perspectives. I have mentioned a few of them in the book, but many others who provided their cooperation a lot go unnamed. I pay my deep acknowledgement from my core of heart to all concerned people to pay their hearty as well as practical help to this book.

And to so many others who have been left unnamed. We are also grateful to the United States of America and United Kingdom of England for their great help from Educational Associations of Management Studies, which provided a management literature, without that nothing was possible. I am also thankful to community of colleagues whose help and advice improved the quality of our thinking and portrayal of this book.

I have described in this book are as follows:

01 Entrepreneur and Entrepreneurship;

02 Empirical Research, Women Entrepreneur;
03 Seventeen most prominent Women Entrepreneurs in India;
04 Female Entrepreneur;
05 Women`s Entrepreneurship Development (WED);
06 Entrepreneurship in Asian Developing Countries;
07 Women Entrepreneurship in India – Opportunities and Challenges;
08 Effective Communication & etc.
09 Female Labour participation in Rural and Urban India;
10 Women and Men in India 2011 & 2012– Highlights;
11 Crime against Women in India;
12 Women`s Work: Has anything Changed?
13 Entrepreneurship development competitive SMEs;
14 Promotion of Women Entrepreneurship;
15 WE- All Women are endowed with Innate Power.

This book seeks to serve as a reliable guide and companion to all employers, Business Owners, HR professionals and all those who are involved directly or indirectly with the businesses of different groups. Although efforts are required for a drastic change in the Management studies in India or in abroad, yet it will still take quite some time to get those proposals translated into reality. With more emphasis on the relationships among Owners, HR professional and workmen, the improvement on organization productivity has not been crossed the appropriate level of the present requirement. In this context I would like to enunciate that the Capitalism or hoarding of resources at the center point it will not do the organization`s problems to be resolved in the near future. Resources are meant for all not for counted people in the segment of businesses or with some Temple Estates, so called Gurus and so many types of property hoarders which are becoming gorgeously richer and richer and our poverty stricken people are in dearth of even two loaves of bread a day.

At one place, abundance of lavishness and aristocracy is prevailed and at another, there is nothing to be pulled on their life. This ingratitude must be worn out from the society of India. Now days, few people are busy with the hoarding of the cash and kind from all means. They don`t have any thinking behind it that how the rest of the population will survive even with appropriate needs of the survival.

That is why the need to know the rudimentary rules and rubrics of law for all, as these is necessary. Much has been changing in general laws but nothing we find in shape of progress and prosperity. The basic tenet and underpinning philosophy of general laws is to protect the interests of the people by saving them from exploitation and harassment on one hand and providing enough leverage and stick of good governance to the Government so as to have concrete art of living culture on the other hand. The cordial and congenial relationship can be had only when both the limbs of society have better understanding in the light of the limits of their rights, responsibilities and duties.

As stated ibid, they are something serious rather than contextual but everything is fair in LOVE and WAR. Here love is for the public of India and war is against the cruel people of society who are behaving like blackcaps of India.

Most of the Indian professionals are unable to forget work while on a holiday, working up to three hours instead of enjoying the free time with family and friends. Developments in technology mean that workers are always connected and the temptation to check emails and complete any tasks that follow on from them is easy to succumb to.

It does not matter that only a few in each generation will grasp and achieve the full reality of man`s proper stature—and that the rest will betray it. It is those few that move the world and give life its meaning—and it is these few that have always sought to address. The rest are no concern of mine; it is not me or all others that they will betray: it is their own souls.

Now, it is, I am hoping in very compassionate way that this book will be proved to be in positive manner, boon for the readers.

2013 **Krishna Kumar Singh**

FOREWORD

Women owned businesses are highly increasing in the economies of almost all countries. The hidden entrepreneurial potentials of women have gradually been changing with the growing sensitivity to the role and economic status in the society. Skill, knowledge and adaptability in business are the main reasons for women to emerge into business ventures. 'Women Entrepreneur' is a person who accepts challenging role to meet her personal needs and become economically independent. A strong desire to do something positive is an inbuilt quality of entrepreneurial women, who is capable of contributing values in both family and social life. With the advent of media, women are aware of their own traits, rights and also the work situations. The glass ceilings are shattered and women are found indulged in every line of business from pappad to power cables. The challenges and opportunities provided to the women of digital era are growing rapidly that the job seekers are turning into job creators. They are flourishing as designers, interior decorators, exporters, publishers, garment manufacturers and still exploring new avenues of economic participation. In India, although women constitute the majority of the total population, the entrepreneurial world is still a male dominated one. Women in advanced nations are recognized and are more prominent in the business world. But the Indian women entrepreneurs are facing some major constraints like –

a) Lack of confidence – In general, women lack confidence in their strength and competence. The family members and the society are reluctant to stand beside their entrepreneurial growth. To a certain extent, this situation is changing among Indian women and yet to face a tremendous change to increase the rate of growth in entrepreneurship.

b) Socio-cultural barriers – Women's family and personal obligations are sometimes a great barrier for succeeding in business career. Only few women are able to manage both home and business efficiently, devoting enough time to perform all their responsibilities in priority.

c) Market-oriented risks – Stiff competition in the market and lack of mobility of women make the dependence of women entrepreneurs on middleman indispensable. Many business women find it difficult to capture the market and make their products popular. They are not fully aware of the changing market conditions and hence can effectively utilize the services of media and internet.

d) Motivational factors – Self motivation can be realized through a mind set for a successful business, attitude to take up risk and behavior towards the business society by shouldering the social responsibilities. Other factors are family support, Government policies, financial assistance from public and private institutions and also the environment suitable for women to establish business units.

e) Knowledge in Business Administration – Women must be educated and trained constantly to acquire the skills and knowledge in all the functional areas of business management. This can facilitate women to excel in decision making process and develop a good business network

f) Awareness about the financial assistance – Various institutions in the financial sector extend their maximum support in the form of incentives, loans, schemes etc. Even then every woman entrepreneur may not be aware of all the assistance provided by the institutions. So the sincere efforts taken towards women entrepreneurs may not reach the entrepreneurs in rural and backward areas.

g) Exposed to the training programs - Training programs and workshops for every type of entrepreneur is available through the social and welfare associations, based on duration, skill and the purpose of the training program. Such programs are really useful to new, rural and young entrepreneurs who want to set up a small and medium scale unit on their own.

h) Identifying the available resources – Women are hesitant to find out the access to cater their needs in the financial and marketing areas. In spite of the mushrooming growth of associations, institutions, and the schemes from the government side, women are not enterprising and dynamic to optimize the resources in the form of reserves, assets mankind or business volunteers.

Highly educated, technically sound and professionally qualified women should be encouraged for managing their own business, rather than dependent on wage employment outlets. The unexplored talents of young women can be identified, trained and used for various types of industries to increase the productivity in the industrial sector. A desirable environment is necessary for every woman to inculcate entrepreneurial values and involve greatly in business dealings.

Contents

1
ENTREPRENEUR

Definition

Someone who exercises initiative by organizing a venture to take benefit of an opportunity and, as the decision maker, decides what, how, and how much of a good or service will be produced.

An entrepreneur supplies risk capital as a risk taker, and monitors and controls the business activities. The entrepreneur is usually a sole proprietor, a partner, or the one who owns the majority of shares in an incorporated venture. According to economist Joseph Alois Schumpeter entrepreneurs are not necessarily motivated by profit but regard it as a standard for measuring achievement.

Schumpeter discovered that they

(1) Greatly value self-reliance,

(2) strive for distinction through excellence,

(3) are highly optimistic and

(4) Always favor challenges of mediumrisk.

Here's the best definition of an entrepreneur I've ever heard:

"Entrepreneurs are people who are too naive to see the obstacles that are obvious to others".

Entrepreneur

The term entrepreneur is a loanword from French, and is commonly used to describe an individual who organizes and operates a business or businesses, taking on financial risk to do so. The term was first defined by the Irish-French economist Richard Cantillon as the person who pays a certain price for a product to resell it at an uncertain price, thereby making decisions about obtaining and using the resources while consequently admitting the risk of enterprise. The term first appeared in the French Dictionary "Dictionnaire Universel de Commerce" of Jacques des Bruslons.

Over time, scholars have defined the term in different ways. Here are some prominent definitions.

- 1803: Jean-Baptiste Say: An entrepreneur is an economic agent who unites all means of production- land of one, the labour of another and the capital of yet another and thus produces a product. By selling the product in the market he pays rent of land, wages to labour, interest on capital and what remains is his profit. He shifts economic resources out of an area of lower and into an area of higher productivity and greater yield.
- 1934: Schumpeter: Entrepreneurs are innovators who use a process of shattering the status quo of the existing products and services, to set up new products, new services.
- 1961: David McClelland: An entrepreneur is a person with a high need for achievement. He is energetic and a moderate risk taker.
- 1964: Peter Drucker: An entrepreneur searches for change, responds to it and exploits opportunities. Innovation is a specific tool of an entrepreneur hence an effective entrepreneur converts a source into a resource.
- 1971: Kilby: Emphasizes the role of an imitator entrepreneur who does not innovate but imitates technologies innovated by others. Are very important in developing economies.
- 1975: Albert Shapero: Entrepreneurs take initiative, accept risk of failure and have an internal locus of control.

- 1975: Howard Stevenson: Entrepreneurship is "the pursuit of opportunity without regard to resources currently controlled."
- 1983: G. Pinchot: Intrapreneur is an entrepreneur within an already established organization.
- 1985: W.B. Gartner: Entrepreneur is a person who started a new business where there was none before.

Women Entrepreneurs

Objectives

This was planned with the following objectives:

- To portray a profile of women entrepreneurs and their enterprises in the small scale sector;
- To explore gender differences in entrepreneurial characteristics;
- To identify problems unique to women in setting up and running their enterprises;
- To document existing policies, programmes, institutional networks and the involvement of support agencies in promoting women's entrepreneurship.

Methodology

An extensive literature review of secondary data sources was undertaken as relevant to the stated objectives of the study.

In order to fill in secondary data gaps on topics such as employment, investment and sector wise distribution of women entrepreneurs, raw data was obtained from 14 States from the Offices of the Development Commissioner (SSI), Government of India. To supplement data obtained from secondary sources, a few case studies were obtained and incorporated in the report.

This study has been conducted within a short time frame. Thus the scope of the study is limited. Since secondary sources of data were relied upon it was difficult to maintain uniformity in sample size for comparative analyses of various aspects related to women entrepreneurs. Also, qualitative analysis has been used in the main, to arrive at conclusions rather than rigorous statistical analyses.

Influences and characteristics of entrepreneurial behavior

Management skill and strong team building abilities are often perceived as essential leadership attribute for successful entrepreneurs. Robert B. Reich considers leadership, management ability and team-building as essential qualities of an entrepreneur.

Psychological studies show that the psychological propensities for male and female entrepreneurs are more similar than different. A growing body of work shows that entrepreneurial behavior is dependent on social and economic factors. Countries with healthy and diversified labor markets or stronger safety nets show a more favorable ratio of opportunity-driven rather than necessity-driven women entrepreneurs. Empirical studies suggest that male entrepreneurs possess strong negotiating skills and consensus-forming abilities.

Research explores the characteristics and personality traits of, and influences on, the entrepreneur have come to differing conclusions. Most, however, agree on certain consistent entrepreneurial traits and environmental influences. Although certain entrepreneurial traits are required, entrepreneurial behaviours are also dynamic and influenced by environmental factors. Shane and Venkataraman argue that the entrepreneur is solely concerned with opportunity recognition and exploitation, although the opportunity that is recognised depends on the type of entrepreneur; while Ucbasaran argue there are many different types contingent upon environmental and personal circumstances.

Jesper Sørensen has argued that some of the most significant influences on an individual's decision to become an entrepreneur are workplace peers and the social composition of the workplace. In researching the likelihood of becoming an entrepreneur based upon working with former entrepreneurs, Sørensen discovered a correlation between working with former entrepreneurs and how often these individuals become entrepreneurs themselves, compared to those who did not work with entrepreneurs. The social composition of the workplace can influence entrepreneurism in workplace peers by proving a possibility for success, causing a "He can do it, why can't I?" attitude. As Sørensen stated, "When you meet others who have gone out on their own, it doesn't seem that crazy."

Perception of entrepreneurs

The ability of entrepreneurs to innovate is thought to relate to innate traits such as extroversion and a proclivity for risk-taking. According to Schumpeter, the capabilities of innovating, introducing new technologies, increasing efficiency and productivity, or generating new products or services, are characteristic qualities of entrepreneurs. Entrepreneurs are catalysts for economic change, and researchers argue that entrepreneurs are highly creative individuals with a tendency to imagine new solutions by finding opportunities for profit or reward. Largely due to the influence of Schumpeter's heroic conceptions of entrepreneurs, it is widely maintained that entrepreneurs are unusual individuals. In line with this view, there is an emerging research tradition investigating the genetic factors that are perceived to make entrepreneurs so distinctive.

However, there are also critical perspectives that attribute these research attitudes to oversimplified methodological and/or philosophical assumptions. It has been argued that entrepreneurs are not that distinctive, but that it is in essence unrealistic preconceptions about "non-entrepreneurs" that maintain laudatory portraits of "entrepreneurs".

Theory-based Typologies

Recent advances in entrepreneur researcher indicate that the differences in entrepreneurs and the heterogeneity in their behaviors and actions can be traced back to their founder's identity. Fauchart and Gruber have recently utilized social identity theory to illustrate that entrepreneurs can be distinguished in three main types- Darwinians, Communitarians and Missionaries. These types of founders not only diverge in fundamental ways in terms of self-views and their social motivations in entrepreneurship, but also engage fairly differently in new firm creation.

Entrepreneurship

Entrepreneurship is the act and art of being an entrepreneur or one who undertakes innovations or introducing new things, finance and business acumen in an effort to transform innovations into economic goods. This may result in new organizations in response to a perceived opportunity. The most obvious form of entrepreneurship is that of starting new businesses; however, in recent years, the term has been extended to include social and political forms of entrepreneurial activity. When entrepreneurship is describing activities within a firm or large organization it is referred to as intra-preneurship and may include corporate venturing, when large entities spin-off organizations.

According to Paul Reynolds, entrepreneurship scholar and creator of the Global Entrepreneurship Monitor, "by the time they reach their retirement years, half of all working men in the United States probably have a period of self-employment of one or more years; one in four may have engaged in self-employment for six or more years. Participating in a new business creation is a common activity among U.S. workers over the course of their careers." And in recent years has been documented by scholars such as David Audretsch to be a major driver of economic growth in both the United States and Western Europe. "As well, entrepreneurship may be defined as the pursuit of opportunity without regard to resources currently controlled."

Entrepreneurial activities are substantially different depending on the type of organization and creativity involved. Entrepreneurship ranges in scale from solo projects to major undertakings creating many job opportunities. Many "high value" entrepreneurial ventures seek venture capital or angel funding in order to raise capital to build the business. Angel investors generally seek annualized returns of 20-30% and more, as well as extensive involvement in the business. Many kinds of organizations now exist to support would-be entrepreneurs including specialized government agencies, business incubators, science parks, and some NGOs. In more recent times, the term entrepreneurship has been extended to include elements not related necessarily to business formation activity such as conceptualizations of entrepreneurship as a specific mindset resulting in entrepreneurial initiatives.

History

The entrepreneur is a factor in microeconomics, and the study of entrepreneurship reaches back to the work of Richard Cantillon and Adam Smith in the late 17th and early 18th centuries, but was largely ignored theoretically until the late 19th and early 20th centuries and empirically until a profound resurgence in business and economics in the last 40 years.

In the 20th century, the understanding of entrepreneurship owes much to the work of economist Joseph Schumpeter in the 1930s and other Austrian economists such as Carl Menger, Ludwig von Mises and Friedrich von Hayek.

Schumpeter

In accordance with Schumpeter, an entrepreneur is a person who is willing and able to convert a new idea or invention into a successful innovation. Entrepreneurship employs what Schumpeter called "the gale of creative destruction" to replace in whole or in part inferior innovations across markets and industries, simultaneously creating new products including new business models. In this way, creative destruction is largely responsible for the dynamism of industries and long-run economic growth. The supposition that entrepreneurship leads to economic growth is an interpretation of the residual in endogenous growth theory and as such is hotly debated in academic economics. An alternate description posited by Israel Kirzner suggests that the majority of innovations may be much more incremental improvements such as the replacement of paper with plastic in the construction of a drinking straw.

For Schumpeter, entrepreneurship resulted in new industries but also in new combinations of currently existing inputs. Schumpeter's initial example of this was the combination of a steam engine and then current wagon making technologies to produce the horseless carriage. In this case the innovation, the car, was transformational but did not require the development of a new technology, merely the application of existing technologies in a novel manner. It did not immediately replace the horsedrawn carriage, but in time, incremental improvements which reduced the cost and improved the technology led to the complete practical replacement of beast drawn vehicles in modern transportation. Despite Schumpeter's early 20th-century contributions, traditional microeconomic theory did not formally consider the entrepreneur in its theoretical frameworks. In this treatment the entrepreneur was an implied but unspecified actor, but it is consistent with the concept of the entrepreneur being the agent of x-efficiency.

Different scholars have described entrepreneurs as, among other things, bearing risk. For Schumpeter, the entrepreneur did not bear risk: the capitalist did.

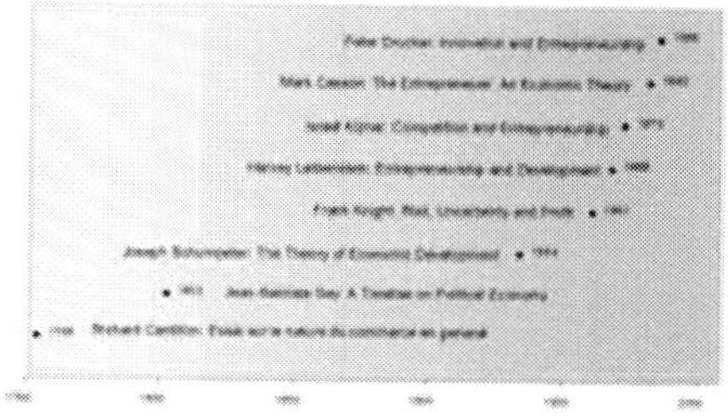

Some notable persons and their works in entrepreneurship history

Knight and Drucker

Frank H. Knight and Peter Drucker defined entrepreneurship is about taking risk. The behavior of the entrepreneur reflects a kind of person willing to put his or her career and financial security on the line and take risks in the name of an idea, spending much time as well as capital on an uncertain venture.

Knight classified three types of uncertainty.

- Risk, which is measurable statistically.
- Ambiguity, which is hard to measure statistically.
- True Uncertainty or Knightian Uncertainty, which is impossible to estimate or predict statistically.

The acts of entrepreneurship are often associated with true uncertainty, particularly when it involves bringing something really novel to the world, whose market never exists. However, even if a market already exists, there is no guarantee that a market exists for a particular new player in the cola category.

The place of the disharmony-creating and idiosyncratic entrepreneur in traditional economic theory presents theoretic quandaries. William Baumol has added greatly to this area of economic theory and was recently honored for it at the 2006 annual meeting of the American Economic Association.

The entrepreneur is widely regarded as an integral player in the business culture of American life, and particularly as an engine for job creation and economic growth. Robert Sobel Zoltan Acs and David Audretsch have produced an edited volume surveying Entrepreneurship as an academic field of research, and more than a hundred scholars around the world track entrepreneurial activity, policy and social influences as part of the Global Entrepreneurship Monitor (GEM) and its associated reports.

Characteristics of an entrepreneur

Entrepreneurs have many of the same character traits as leaders, similar to the early great man theories of leadership; however trait-based theories of entrepreneurship are increasingly being called into question. Entrepreneurs are often contrasted with managers and administrators who are said to be more methodical and less prone to risk-taking. Such person-centric models of entrepreneurship have shown to be of questionable validity, not least as many real-life entrepreneurs operate in teams rather than as single individuals. Still, a vast literature studying the entrepreneurial personality argues that certain traits seem to be associated with entrepreneurs:

- **Bird** - mercurial, that is, prone to insights, brainstorms, deceptions, ingeniousness and resourcefulness. They are cunning, opportunistic, creative, and unsentimental.
- **Busenitz and Barney** - prone to overconfidence and over generalizations.
- **Cole** - found there are four types of entrepreneur: the innovator, the calculating inventor, the over-optimistic promoter, and the organization builder. These types are not

related to the personality but to the type of opportunity the entrepreneur faces.

- **Collins and Moore** - tough, pragmatic people driven by needs of independence and achievement. They seldom are willing to submit to authority.
- **Cooper, Woo, & Dunkelberg** - argue that entrepreneurs exhibit extreme optimism in their decision-making processes.
- **John Howkins** - focused specifically on creative entrepreneurship. He found that entrepreneurs in the creative industries needed a specific set of traits including the ability to prioritise ideas over data, to be nomadic and to learn endlessly.
- **David McClelland** - primarily motivated by an overwhelming need for achievement and strong urges to build.

Concept

It has assumed super importance for accelerating economic growth both in developed and developing countries. It promotes capital formation and creates wealth in country. It is hope and dreams of millions of individuals around the world. It reduces unemployment and poverty and it is a pathway to prosper. Entrepreneurship is the process of exploring the opportunities in the market place and arranging resources required to exploit these opportunities for long term gain. It is the process of planning, organizing, opportunities and assuming. Thus it is a risk of business enterprise. It may be distinguished as an ability to take risk independently to make utmost earnings in the market. It is a creative and innovative skill and adapting response to environment.

Promotion

Entrepreneurship's potential to support economic growth; it is the policy goal of many governments to develop a culture of entrepreneurial thinking. This can be done in a number of ways: by integrating entrepreneurship into education systems, legislating to encourage risk-taking, and national campaigns.

Many of the initiatives have been brought together under the umbrella of Global Entrepreneurship Week, a worldwide celebration and promotion of youth entrepreneurship, which started in 2008.

Financial Bootstrapping

Financial bootstrapping is a term used to cover different methods for avoiding using the financial resources of external investors. Bootstrapping can be defined as "a collection of methods used to minimize the amount of outside debt and equity financing needed from banks and investors" The use of private credit card debt is the most known form of bootstrapping, but a wide variety of methods are available for entrepreneurs. While bootstrapping involves a risk for the founders, the absence of any other stakeholder gives the founders more freedom to develop the company. Many successful companies including Dell Computers and Facebook were founded this way.

There are different types of bootstrapping:

- Owner financing
- Sweat equity
- Minimization of the accounts payable
- Joint utilization
- Delaying payment
- Minimizing inventory
- Subsidy finance
- Personal Debt

External financing

Many businesses need more capital than can be provided by the owners themselves, and in this case a range of options are available including:

- Angel investors
- Venture capital investors.
- Crowd funding
- Hedge funds
- Alternative Asset Management

Some of this source provides not only funds, but also financial oversight, accountability for carrying out tasks and meeting milestones, and in some cases business contacts and experience - in many cases in return for an equity stake.

Women Entrepreneurs Law & Legal Definition

Women entrepreneur is any women who organizes and manages any enterprise, especially a business.

As of 2002, there were 6.5 million majority women-owned businesses in the United States, employing 7.1 million people according to the U.S. Bureau of the Census. The number of privately held women-owned businesses in U.S. exceeds 10 million if one counts partially women-owned businesses as well. According to a Business Week Online article, "between 1997 and 2004 the number of women-owned companies grew 28.1 percent—nearly three times the rate of all privately held businesses." These statistics reflect a sea change in American conceptions of gender roles and abilities over the past half-century.

Women have owned and operated businesses for decades, but they were not always recognized or given credit for their efforts. Often women entrepreneurs were "invisible" as they worked side by side with their husbands, and many only stepped into visible leadership positions when their husbands died. But a variety of factors have combined in recent years to contribute to the visibility and number of women who start their own businesses. According to U.S. Department of Labor statistics, female participation in the workforce was less than 40 percent in 1960 but is predicted to reach 62 percent by the year 2015. As women enter the workforce in ever-greater numbers, they gain professional experience, and managerial skills, both necessary to be successful entrepreneurs. Flexibility is also a factor in many women's decision to start a business. Entrepreneurship is often seen as an ideal way to juggle the competing demands of career and family. Finally, the disparity in the salaries and wages that women earn as compared to men on average has been a factor in motivating some women to decide to establish their own businesses.

Although the small businesses owned by women have traditionally been in the service sector, in recent years women entrepreneurs have been moving rapidly into manufacturing, construction, and other industrial fields. Women business owners still face greater difficulties in gaining access to commercial credit and bidding on government contracts than do their male colleagues, and pockets of resistance to women entrepreneurs remain strong in some industries and geographic regions. But millions of successful businesses launched and managed by women now dot America's business landscape, each a testament to the legitimacy of the aspirations and talents of the woman entrepreneur.

Reasons Women Become Entrepreneurs

Many studies indicate that women start businesses for fundamentally different reasons than their male counterparts. While men start businesses primarily for growth opportunities and profit potential, women most often found businesses in order to meet personal goals, such as gaining feelings of achievement and accomplishment. In many instances, women consider financial success as an external confirmation of their ability rather than as a primary goal or motivation to start a business, although millions of women entrepreneurs will grant that financial profitability is important in its own right.

Women also tend to start businesses about ten years later than men, on average. Motherhood, lack of management experience, and traditional socialization has all been cited as reasons for delayed entry into entrepreneurial careers. Many women start a business due to some traumatic event, such as divorce, discrimination due to pregnancy or the corporate glass ceiling, the health of a family member, or economic reasons such as a layoff. But a new talent pool of women entrepreneurs is forming today, as more women opt to leave corporate America to chart their own destinies. These women have developed financial expertise and bring experience in manufacturing or nontraditional fields. As a result, the concentration of women business owners in the retail and service sectors—and in traditional industries such as cosmetics, food, fashion, and personal care—is slowly changing.

Problems faced by Women Entrepreneurs

One of the main problems facing women entrepreneurs is obtaining financing. In the early 1990s, study after study confirmed that women business owners did not receive equal treatment at financial institutions. Over one half of women business owners believed that they faced gender discrimination when dealing with a loan officer. And for women, venture capital firms appear to show the same favoritism towards men that banks do. According to Sona Wang, quoted in a Crain's Chicago Business article and general partner of Inroads Capital Partners, was an Evanston venture capital firm that specializes in backing women and minorities, the venture capital business "clearly relies heavily on the old-boy network." Only 5 percent of the companies that received venture capital funding in 2004 had a female CEO, according to the Crain's Chicago Business article, a trend that has not changed since researchers started tracking these numbers in 1997.

In an effort to bring more equity into the capital acquisitions area, the Small Business Administration's Women's

Prequalification Pilot Loan Program was developed. Introduced in 1994 and expanded nationwide in 1997, the program helps women seeking loans of under $250,000 to complete their loan applications, and also provides an SBA guarantee for repayment of their loans. Women are prequalified based on their character, credit rating, and ability to repay the loan from future business earnings, rather than on collateral. The prequalification statement from the SBA enables the women to obtain funding much more readily.

Another area in which women business owners have been historically shortchanged is procurement, or the selling of their goods and services to city, state, and federal governments. In the past, fewer than 5 percent of the women-owned firms in the United States were certified to do business with their state government and only 1.5 percent of the billions of dollars in federal contracts went to women-owned firms. Some efforts have been undertaken to rectify this situation. If a company is 51 percent owned and controlled by a woman, it can obtain certification and bid on government contracts. In addition, many government agencies at the state and federal levels have created set-aside programs that specifically help women-owned businesses in the bidding process. Nonetheless, the percentage of government contracts going to women-owned firms remained a meager 3 percent as recently as 2002.

Resources

A number of resources now exist to support women entrepreneurs. In 1988, Congress authorized the Small Business Administration Office of Women's Business Ownership, which created a "Low-Doc" loan program which makes it easier for women entrepreneurs to obtain SBA financing. The SBA also has established a Women's Network for Entrepreneurial Training (WNET) which links women mentors with protegees.

Small Business Development Centers (SBDC) are also co-sponsored by the SBA and operate in every state. They offer free and confidential counseling to anyone interested in starting a small business. In addition, many states now have a Women's Business Advocate to promote women entrepreneurs within the state. These advocates are represented by an organization, the National Association of Women Business Advocates.

A number of trade associations also represent women entrepreneurs. The National Association of Women Business Owners is the largest group throughout the country. There are also some smaller regional groups, which can be located through the Yellow Pages or local chambers of commerce. The American Business Women's Association provides leadership, networking, and educational support. The National Association of Female Executives makes women aware of the need to plan for career and financial success. As women-owned businesses continue to create jobs and become an increasingly important factor in the American economy, the resources to support them will continue to grow as well.

National Association of Women Business Owners (NAWBO Announces Its 2012-2013 Board of Directors

The National Association of Women Business Owners (NAWBO) is proud to announce the installation of its new 2012-2013 Board of Directors.

"Each of these dynamic, entrepreneurial women bring unique talents and value to NAWBO and will be a powerful force as we continue to advocate on behalf of women business owners in the nation's capital," says NAWBO® President and CEO Diane Tomb . "In addition, they will share their business acumen and experience to support our membership around the country as we continue to grow and provide resources for women business owners to expand their businesses to the next level. As women business owners continue to be the fastest growing sector of the economy and will be the job creators of the next decade, there's never been a more exciting time for NAWBO® and our Board of Directors."

The 2012-2013 Board will be formally introduced to the business community at NAWBO's Women's Business Conference 2012, held October 4th-5th at the Louisville Marriott Downtown in Louisville, Kentucky. For more information on the conference,

The new Board is headed by National Chair Laura Yamanaka, president and founder of teamCFO, Inc. in Los Angeles, California. The firm partners with small and midsize businesses to improve company performance and growth by providing quality financial accounting consulting services. Yamanaka is a past president of NAWBO®-Los Angeles and a long-time champion of financial literacy for women business owners.

Congratulations to the entire 2012-2013 NAWBO Board of Directors:

Officers	
President & Ceo **Diane Tomb** Nawbo Washington, Dc	Chair-Elect **Billie Dragoo** Repucare Indianapolis, In
Chair **Laura Yamanaka** Teamcfo, Inc. Los Angeles, Ca	Immediate Past Chair **Evelyn Strange** Advanced Electrical Systems, Inc. Louisville, Ky

Secretary/Treasurer **Deborah Stallings** Hr Anew, Inc. Columbia, Md	
Directors	
Renee White Fraser, Ph.D. Fraser Communications Los Angeles, Ca	Chair, Presidents Assembly **Lola Kakes** Effortlesshr, Inc. Tuscon, Az
Teresa Meares Dgg Taser And Tactical Supply Jacksonville, Fl	
Dana Rambow Aristocare Home Health Services Tucson, Az	
Crystal Arredondo Mpact Financial Group Dallas, Tx	

About NAWBO

Founded in 1975, NAWBO® is the voice of America's more than 10 million women-owned businesses. By representing the interests of women entrepreneurs across various industries from state capitals to our nation's capital, NAWBO® strives to advocate on behalf of women business owners on matters of public policy as well as develop programs to navigate women entrepreneurs through the various stages of business growth and provide networking opportunities where members can share best practices. Learn more at nawbo.org.

With the changing colors and schedules quickly turning from relaxed to full gear, your NAWBO Board has been busy planning the 2012-2013 year. This year our theme is "Focusing On Your Bottom Line" and we intend to help you do just that. As the economy continues to struggle from the economic downturn of the past few years, women business owners are emerging in record numbers. This segment of the business community is a relevant force in the recovery.

So what do we have planned? Our first networking event will be a repeat of our successful Wine Tasting at LL Dent Restaurant on October 9, 2012. Come out and enjoy Long Island Pindar Wines and fabulous southern style appetizers while catching up with friends old and new.

We then turn our attention to subjects that include maximizing your cash flow, sales training, and doing business with the government. We will keep you informed of complimentary information such as Expos that are pertinent to what we are all trying to accomplish.

This organization has been supporting women business owners for over twenty five years and we are looking forward to the next twenty five. We have had some wonderful success stories and I have had the privilege of working with many inspiring women.

Kalpana Patel led this organization for two years as President culminating in an outstanding Twenty-Fifth Anniversary Gala that highlighted twenty five women of distinction in numerous fields. Her tenacity and dedication to our organization has benefitted many women in their quest for a successful business. She was succeeded by our Immediate Past President, Linda Agnew who continued to work on getting our message out and strengthening the core of our organization to everyone's benefit. The board is comprised of successful women in many areas of business all with the same passion to secure that all women have the opportunity to grow and flourish.

We look forward to continuing to grow together this year and into the future. Remember NAWBO Long Island is here for all of us, so if you have a suggestion that could help - let us know. If you know someone who may benefit from our organization introduce them to one of our events.

2
Empirical Research

Empirical research is a way of gaining knowledge by means of direct and indirect observation or experience. Empirical evidence can be analyzed quantitatively or qualitatively. Through quantifying the evidence or making sense of it in qualitative form, a researcher can answer empirical questions, which should be clearly defined and answerable with the evidence collected. Research design varies by field and by the question being investigated. Many researchers combine qualitative and quantitative forms of analysis to better answer questions which cannot be studied in laboratory settings, particularly in the social sciences and in education.

In some fields, quantitative research may begin with a research question which is tested through experimentation in a lab. Usually, a researcher has a certain theory regarding the topic under investigation. Based on this theory some statements, or hypotheses, will be proposed. From these hypotheses predictions about specific events are derived. These predictions can then be tested with a suitable experiment. Depending on the outcomes of the experiment, the theory on which the hypotheses and predictions were based will be supported or not.

Terminology

The term empirical was originally used to refer to certain ancient Greek practitioners of medicine who rejected adherence to the dogmatic doctrines of the day, preferring instead to rely on the observation of phenomena as perceived in experience. Later empiricism referred to a theory of knowledge in philosophy which adheres to the principle that knowledge arises from experience and evidence gathered specifically using the senses. In scientific use the term empirical refers to the gathering of data using only evidence that is observable by the senses or in some cases using calibrated scientific instruments. What early philosophers described as empiricist and empirical research have in common is the dependence on observable data to formulate and test theories and come to conclusions.

Usage

The researcher attempts to describe accurately the interaction between the instrument and the entity being observed. If instrumentation is involved, the researcher is expected to calibrate his/her instrument by applying it to known standard objects and documenting the results before applying it to unknown objects. In other words, it describes the research that has not taken place before and their results.

In practice, the accumulation of evidence for or against any particular theory involves planned research designs for the collection of empirical data, and academic rigor plays a large part of judging the merits of research design. Several typographies for such designs have been suggested, one of the most popular of which comes from Campbell and Stanley. They are responsible for popularizing the widely cited distinction among pre-experimental, experimental, and quasi-experimental designs and are staunch advocates of the central role of randomized experiments in educational research.

Scientific research

Accurate analysis of data using standardized statistical methods in scientific studies is critical to determining the validity of empirical research. Statistical formulas such as regression, uncertainty coefficient, t-test, chi square, and various types of ANOVA are fundamental to forming logical, valid conclusions. If empirical data reach significance under the appropriate statistical formula, the research hypothesis is supported. If not, the null hypothesis is supported, meaning no effect of the independent variables was observed on the dependent variables.

It is important to understand that the outcome of empirical research using statistical hypothesis testing is never proof. It can only support a hypothesis, reject it, or do neither. These methods yield only probabilities.

Among scientific researchers, empirical evidence refers to objective evidence that appears the same regardless of the observer. A thermometer will not display different temperatures for each individual who observes it. Temperature, as measured by an accurate, well calibrated thermometer, is empirical evidence. By contrast, non-empirical evidence is subjective, depending on the observer. Following the previous example, observer A might truthfully report that a room is warm, while observer B might truthfully report that the same room is cool, though both observe the same reading on the thermometer. The use of empirical evidence negates this effect of personal experience.

Empirical cycle

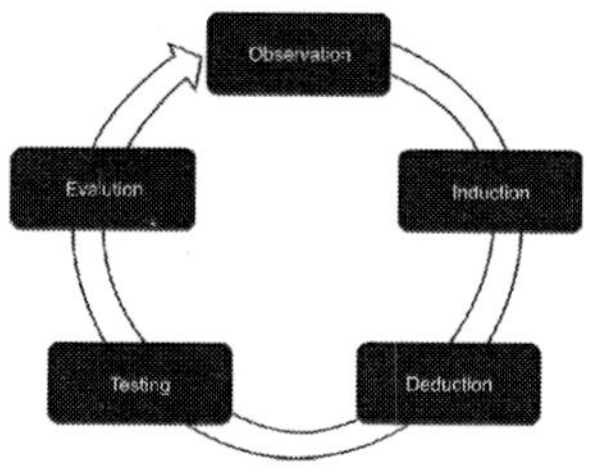

Empirical cycle according to A.D. de Groot

Trait theory

In psychology, **trait theory** is an approach to the study of human personality. Trait theorists are primarily interested in the measurement of traits, which can be defined as habitual patterns of behavior, thought, and emotion. According to this perspective, traits are relatively stable over time, differ across individuals, and influence behavior.

Gordon Allport was an early pioneer in the study of traits, which he sometimes referred to as dispositions. In his approach, central traits are basic to an individual's personality, whereas secondary traits are more peripheral. Common traits are those recognized within a culture and may vary between cultures. Cardinal traits are those by which an individual may be strongly recognized. Since Allport's time, trait theorists have focused more on group statistics than on single individuals. Allport called these two emphases "nomothetic" and "idiographic," respectively.

There are a nearly unlimited number of potential traits that could be used to describe personality. The statistical technique of factor analysis, however, has demonstrated that particular clusters of traits reliably correlate together. Hans Eysenck has suggested that personality is reducible to three major traits. Other researchers argue that more factors are needed to adequately describe human personality including humor, wealth and beauty. Many psychologists currently believe that five factors are sufficient.

Virtually all trait models, and even ancient Greek philosophy, include extraversion vs. introversion as a central dimension of human personality. Another prominent trait that is found in nearly all models is Neuroticism, or emotional instability.

The Two taxonomies

Both approaches extensively use self-report questionnaires. The factors are intended to be orthogonal, though there are often small positive correlations between factors. The five factor model in particular has been criticized for losing the orthogonal structure between factors. Hans Eysenck has argued that fewer factors are superior to a larger number of partly related ones. Although these two approaches are comparable because of the use of factor analysis to construct hierarchical taxonomies, they differ in the organization and number of factors.

Whatever the causes, however, psychoticism marks the two approaches apart, as the five factor model contains no such trait. Moreover, psychoticism, unlike any of the other factors in either approach, does not fit a normal distribution curve. Indeed, scores are rarely high, thus skewing a normal distribution. However, when they are high, there is considerable overlap with psychiatric conditions such as antisocial and schizoid personality disorders. Similarly, high scorers on neuroticism are more susceptible to sleep and psychosomatic disorders. Five factor approaches can also predict future mental disorders.

Lower-order factors

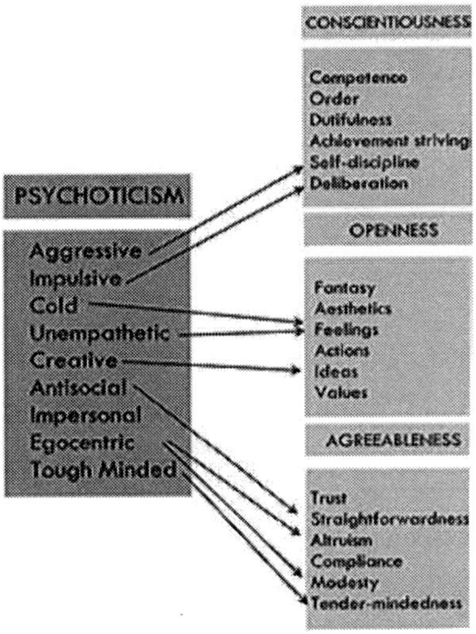

There are similarities between lower-order factors for psychoticism and the facets of openness, agreeableness, and conscientiousness.

There are two higher-order factors that both taxonomies clearly share: extraversion and neuroticism. Both approaches broadly accept that extraversion is associated with sociability and positive effect, whereas neuroticism is associated with emotional instability and negative effect.

Many lower-order factors, or facets, are similar between the two taxonomies. Both approaches contain factors for gregariousness, for activity levels, and for assertiveness within the higher order factor extraversion. However, there are differences too. First, the three-factor approach contains nine lower-order factors and the five-factor approach has six.

Eysenck's psychoticism factor incorporates some of the polar opposites of the lower order factors of openness, agreeableness and conscientiousness. A high scorer on tough-mindedness in psychoticism would score low on tender-mindedness in agreeableness. Most of the differences between the taxonomies stem from the three factor model's emphasis on fewer high-order factors.

Causality

Although both major trait models are descriptive, only the three-factor model offers a detailed causal explanation. Eysenck suggests that different personality traits are caused by the properties of the brain, which they are the results of genetic factors? In particular, the three-factor model identifies the reticular system and the limbic system in the brain as key components that mediate cortical arousal and emotional responses respectively. Eysenck advocates that extraverts have low levels of cortical arousal and introverts have high levels, leading extraverts to seek out more stimulation from socializing and being venturesome. Moreover, Eysenck surmised that there would be an optimal level of arousal, after which inhibition would occur and that this would be different for each person.

In a similar vein, the three-factor approach theorizes that neuroticism is mediated by levels of arousal in the limbic system and that individual differences arise because of variable activation thresholds between people. Therefore, highly neurotic people when presented with minor stressors will exceed this threshold, whereas people low in neuroticism will not exceed normal activation levels, even when presented with large stressors. By contrast, proponents of the five-factor approach assume a role of genetics and environment but offer no explicit causal explanation.

Given this emphasis on biology in the three-factor approach, it would be expected that the third trait, psychoticism, would have a similar explanation. However, the causal properties of this state are not well defined. Eysenck has suggested that psychoticism is related to testosterone levels and is an inverse function of the serotonergic system, but he later revised this, linking it instead to the dopaminergic system.

List of personality traits

Personality Traits	
Openness to experience	Composed of two related but separable traits, Openness to Experience and Intellect. Behavioral aspects include having wide interests and being imaginative and insightful, correlated with activity in the dorsolateral prefrontal cortex. Considered primarily a cognitive trait.
Conscientiousness	Scrupulous, meticulous, principled behavior guided or conforming to one's own conscience. Associated with the dorsolateral prefrontal cortex. Anorexics are noted to have higher levels of conscientiousness.

Extraversion	Gregarious, outgoing, sociable, projecting one's personality outward. The opposite of extraversion is introversion. Extraversion has shown to share certain genetic markers with substance abuse. Extraversion is associated with various regions of the prefrontal cortex and the amygdala.
Agreeableness	Refers to a compliant, trusting, empathic, sympathetic, friendly and cooperative nature.
Neuroticism	"Refers to an individual's tendency to become upset or emotional" "Neuroticism is the major factor of personality pathology." Neuroticism has been linked to serotonin transporter (5-HTT) binding sites in the thalamus: as well as activity in the insular cortex.
Self-esteem (low)	A "favorable or unfavorable attitude toward the self." An individual's sense of his or her value or worth, or the extent to which a person values, approves of, appreciates, prizes, or likes him or herself"
Harm avoidance	A tendency towards shyness, being fearful and uncertain, tendency to worry. Neonatal complications such as preterm birth have been shown to affect harm avoidance. Those with BED, AN, and BN exhibit high levels of harm avoidance. The volume of the left amygdala in girls was correlated to levels of HA, in separate studies HA was correlated with reduced grey matter volume in the orbito-frontal, occipital and parietal regions.

Novelty seeking	Impulsive, exploratory, fickle, excitable, quick-tempered, and extravagant. Associated with addictive behavior.
Perfectionism	"I don't think needing to be perfect is in any way adaptive" (Paul Hewitt) Socially prescribed perfectionism – "believing that others will value you only if you are perfect." Self-oriented perfectionism – "an internally motivated desire to be perfect. Perfectionism is one of the traits associated with obsessional behavior and like obsessionality is also believed to be regulated by the basal ganglia.
Alexithymia	The inability to express emotions. "To have no words for one's inner experience." In studies done with stroke patients, alexithymia was found to be more prevalent in those who developed lesions in the right hemisphere following a cerebral infarction. There is a positive association with post-traumatic stress disorder (PTSD), childhood abuse and neglect and alexithymia. Utilizing psychometric testing and fMRI, studies showed positive response in the insula, posterior cingulate cortex (PCC), and thalamus.
Rigidity	Inflexibility, difficulty making transitions, adherence to set patterns. Mental rigidity arises out of a deficit of the executive functions. Originally termed frontal lobe syndrome it is also referred to as dysexecutive syndrome and usually occurs

as a result of damage to the frontal lobe. This may be due to physical damage, disease or a hypoxic or anoxic insult.

Impulsivity

Risk taking, lack of planning, and making up one's mind quickly. A component of disinhibition. Abnormal patterns of impulsivity have been linked to lesions in the right inferior frontal gyrus and in studies done by Antonio Damasio author of Descartes Error, damage to the ventromedial prefrontal cortex has been shown to cause a defect in real-life decision making in individuals with otherwise normal intellect. Those who sustain this type of damage are oblivious to the future consequences of their actions and live in the here and now.

Disinhibition

Behavioral dis-inhibition is an inability or unwillingness to constrain impulses; it is a key component of executive functioning. Researchers have emphasized poor behavioral inhibition as the central impairment of ADHD. It may be symptomatic of orbitofrontal lobe syndrome, a subtype of frontal lobe syndrome which may be an acquired disorder as a result of traumatic brain injury, hypoxic ischemic encephalopathy (HIE), anoxic encephalopathy, degenerative diseases such as Parkinson's, bacterial or viral infections such as Lyme disease and neurosyphilis. Disinhibition has been consistently associated with substance abuse disorders, obesity, higher BMI, excessive eating, an increased rate of eating, and perceived hunger.

Psychoticism Psychoticism is a personality pattern typified by aggressiveness and interpersonal hostility, one of four traits in Hans Eysenck's model of personality. High levels of this trait were believed by Eysenck to be linked to increased vulnerability to psychosis such as schizophrenia. He also believed that blood relatives of psychotics would show high levels of this trait, suggesting a genetic basis to the trait.

Obsessionality Persistent, often unwelcome, and frequently disturbing ideas, thoughts, images or emotions, rumination, often inducing an anxious state. Obsessionality may result as a dysfunction of the basal ganglia.

Definition of women entrepreneur

Technically, a "women entrepreneur" is any women who organizes and manages any enterprise, esp. a business, usually with considerable initiative and risk.

However, quite often the term "women-owned business" is used relative to government contracting. In this instance, the entrepreneur (a woman) owns (more than 50%), controls and runs the enterprise.

Women Entrepreneurs- Definition

An enterprise owned and controlled by one or more women having a minimum financial holding of 51% or more, giving 51% or more employment to women Some Facts:

Women constitute not only half of the World's population but also sway the growth of the remaining half

- They produce half of the world's food supply

- They account for 60% of the work force
- Own less than 1% of the real estate
- Profile of a typical women entrepreneur
- First born child of middle class parents
- At least one of the parents is self employed
- College educated
- Married
- First significant venture in early 30s
- Previous experience in a new venture
- Desire for independence and job satisfaction
- Self confident and moderate risk taker
- High tolerance for ambiguity
- High energy levels

Start up problems: Obtaining credit, access to information, marketing, lack of experience in financial planning, taxation, cash flow management, personnel management: -

- DIC scheme
- Encouragement to start women entrepreneurship in areas with population of less than Rs. 1 Lakh
- Investment in machinery up to Rs.2 Lakh is allowed
- 20% of this investment is granted as seed capital
- For backward classes, the seed capital is up to 30%
- The interest rate is 4%
- Remaining capital needs to be financed by banks/financial institutions
- Single Window Scheme
- Scheme by SIDBI to provide fixed and working capital from a single source
- Project cost excluding working capital and margin money, can go up to Rs. 20 Lakh
- Repayment period-10 years

  Founder's capital- Minimum 25%

  Mahila Arthik Vikas Mahamandal (MAVIM)

Established on the 24th February, 1975

Schemes:

Maharashtra Rural Credit Programme (MRCP),

SwarnaJayanti Gram Swarozgar Yojana (SGSY),

Swayamsiddha Programme (IWEP),

Mahila Swavalamban Nidhi (MSN),

RamaiMahila Shakshamikaran (SCP),

NABARD Add-On Project,

Rashtriya Samvikas Yojana (RSY),

Krushi Saptak Yojana and

Tribal Development Project (TSP)

Activities/objective: Self employment of women, training them invarious product and service industries, assisting them to start business and manage it

Mahila Udyog Nidhi and Mahila Vikas Nidhi

Started by SIDBI in 1990

Provides finance up to Rs.10 Lakh through state Financing Corporation and SIDC

Financial assistance provided as concessional rate

Mahila Vikas Nidhi also provides assistance in training women entrepreneurs

3

Women Entrepreneurs in India

Seventeen Most Prominent Women Entrepreneurs in India

The educated women do not want to limit their lives in the four walls of the house. They demand equal respect from their partners. However, Indian women have to go a long way to achieve equal rights and position because traditions are deep rooted in Indian society. Despite all the social hurdles, many women have become successful in their works. These successful women have made name & wealth for themselves with their hard work, diligence, competence and will power. Following is the list of few Top Women Entrepreneurs in India:

1) Jessie Paul: With many awards and recognitions in her kitty, such as Chairman's Award, Infosys-1998, Data Quest's list of most powerful women in IT in India, 2005, Business Today's List of Women Achievers in India, 2007, IT People's Award for Women in Leadership-2008, Jessie Paul is currently the CEO of Paul Writer Strategic Advisory, which is a marketing advisory firm and the author of the book No Money Marketing. She has been part of Wipro for four and half years where she created the shared-marketing unit for Wipro Technologies and Wipro InfoTech. Her own company, Paul Writer Strategic Advisory, is a marketing platform for B2B early-stage companies in the traditional and new media space like social blogging. She is considered as an expert in brand globalization.

2) Indra Nooyi: Indian born American businesswoman, Indra Krishnamurthy Nooyi born October 28, 1955 is the Chairperson and Chief Executive Officer (CEO) of PepsiCo.

On August 14, 2006, Nooyi was named the successor to Steven Reinemund as chief executive officer of the company effective October 1, 2006. On February 5, 2007, she was named Chairperson, effective May 2, 2007.

Nooyi joined PepsiCo in 1994 and was named president and CFO in 2001. Nooyi has directed the company's global strategy for more than decade and led PepsiCo's restructuring, including the 1997 divestiture of its restaurants into Tricon, now known as Yum! Brands. Nooyi also took the lead in the acquisition of Tropicana in 1998 and merger with Quaker Oats Company also brought Gatorade to PepsiCo. In 2007 she became the fifth CEO in PepsiCo's 44'year history.

Nooyi's key contributions include promoting and supporting socially responsible business practices, including taking on one of the planet's most pressing problems climate change. Her commitment to global citizenship is evidenced by her multi'year growth strategy, 'Performance with Purpose'.

Nooyi was named on Wall Street Journal's list of 50 women to watch in 2007 and 2008, and was listed among Time's 100 Most Influential People in The World in 2007 and 2008. Nooyi has been named 2009 CEO of the Year by the Global.

3) Dr. Kiran Mazumdar-Shaw: Entrepreneur Dr. Kiran Mazumdar-Shaw, Chairman & Managing Director of Bioon Ltd. She was educated at the Bishop Cotton Girls School and Mount Carmel College in Bangalore.

She founded Biocon India with a capital of Rs.10, 000 in her garage in 1978 – the initial operation was to extract an enzyme from papaya. Her application for loans were turned down by banks then – on three counts – biotechnology was then a new word, the company lacked assets, and women entrepreneurs were still a rarity. Today, her company is the biggest biopharmaceutical firm in the country.

In 2004, Biocon went for an IPO and the issue was over–subscribed by over 30 times. Post–IPO, Shaw held close to 40% of the stock of the company and was regarded as India's richest woman with an estimated worth of Rs. 2,100 crore.

4) Chanda Kochhar: Chanda Kochhar a Masters Degree in Management Studies from Jamnalal Bajaj Institute of Management Studies. She joined ICICI as a Management trainee after her Master in the year 1984. Later she was appointed as part of core team to set the ICICI bank. She became Deputy General Manager in 1996. In 2001, she was promoted as Executive Director, heading the retail business in ICICI Bank. In 2006, she was appointed as the Deputy Managing Director of ICICI bank. She holds many prestigious awards and honors to her credit. She won the Retail Banker of the Year 2004 by the Asian Banker, Business Women of the Year 2005 by The Economic Times and Rising Star Award for Global Awards 2006 by Retail Banker International. She is also been featured in Fortune's list of Most Powerful Women in Business.

5) Neelam Dhawan: The Managing Director of Hewlett-Packard India, Neelam Dhawan has been featured in Fortune's annual global list of '50 Most Powerful Women in Business'-2009 and was ranked No. 37. Like other B-school graduates, she wanted to join

FMCG rather than joining IT. It all happened at Shiv Nadar-promoted HCL Technologies and spent 14 years learning the traits of sales and marketing. Later in 1995, she joined IBM as VP of sales and marketing for another four years.

6) Anu Aga: This woman became the Chairperson of Thermax Engineering after the death of her husband Rohinton Aga. The company's condition was critical at that time. Its share price dipped to Rs. 36 from Rs. 400. Anu Aga, the then Director of Human Resource, Thermax, was compelled to take charge of the company.

In order to make the company profitable, she brought a consultant from abroad and restructured the company. The strategy worked and the company saw profit again. She stepped down from the post of chairperson in 2004. Now, she spends most of her time in social activities. Bombay Management Association awarded her Management Woman Achiever of the Year Award 2002-2003.

After retiring from Thermax, she took to social work, and 2010 was awarded the Padma Shri (Social Work) by Govt. of India.

7) Sulajja Firodia Motwani: Sulajja Firodia Motwani is Joint Managing Director of Kinetic Engineering Ltd. She is also the in charge of the Company's overall business developmental activities.

She is also very well performing the role of the Director of Kinetic Motor Company Limited and Kinetic Marketing Services Limited. She has made an incredible contribution in making the firm reach heights of success.

Prior to joining Kinetic Company, Sulajja worked for a period of four years with a well known investment analytics company, BARRA International, based in California. She has been an active participant in setting the operations of the company in India. Throughout her studies, she has been a rank holder. She has always cleared exams with merit. Her name appeared in the toppers list in the SSC examinations and HSC examinations. She graduated from the Pune University.

Thereafter, she went to the United States for pursuing further studies. She is an MBA degree holder from the reputed Carnegie Mellon University at Pittsburgh.

She is an epitome of boldness and courage. With her strong determination and courage, she has been able to establish a niche for the firm in the business world. The Company has witnessed tremendous expansion during her tenure.

From being a mere moped manufacturer, today, it has set its foothold in the industry as a manufacturer offering a complete range of two wheelers right from mopeds, scooters to motorcycles.

8) Ekta Kapoor: Ekta Kapoor is a creative head of Balajji Telefilms. She is the daughter of actor Jeetendra, and sister of actor Tushar Kapoor. She has been synonymous with the rage of soap operas on Indian TV, after her most famous venture 'Kyunki Saas Bhi Kabhi Bahu Thi', which started airing on STAR Plus in 2000.

Ekta dominates Indian television, producing more than eight television soaps.

At the 6th Indian Telly Awards 2006, she bagged the Hall of Fame award for her contributions. Most of her creations begin with the letter 'K' due to her superstition that it brings her good luck.

She is 'a smart woman with a definite agenda' and has also been appropriately termed as Asia`s most powerful communicator and the lady no.1 in Hindi serials and movies.

9) Simone Tata: With her visions, she changed a small unknown cosmetics company, one of the subsidiaries of Tata Oil Mills, into one of the leading cosmetic companies of India. Lakme changed the face of Indian fashion and cosmetics forever. For her success, Simone N. Tata is also known as Cosmetic Czarina of India. Simone joined Lakme in 1961 and became Chairperson in 1982.

Eyeing growth in the retails sector, in 1996 Tata sold off Lakmé to Hindustan Lever Limited (HLL), and created Trent from the money it made through the sale.

All shareholders of Lakmé were given, equivalent share in Trent. The Westside brand and stores belongs to Trent. Simone Tata was the wife of late Naval H. Tata and is step mother to Ex-Tata group chairman Sri Ratan Naval Tata.

10) Vidya Manohar Chhabria: The wife of late Manohar Rajaram Chhabria, is now leading Jumbo Group, a Dubai based \$1.5 billion business conglomerate. She became chairperson of the company after the death of her husband in 2002. She runs the business with the help of her three daughters. She was ranked 38th most powerful women by the Fortune magazine in 2003.

The interests of the Jumbo Group include consumer electronics and durables, tyres and tubes, brewing and distilling products, chemicals, machinery and equipment. The group's Indian companies have interests in brewing and supply-chain management.

She manages to also attend to household chores and spend time with her daughters. A great lover of Indian cuisine and music, at present, her dream is to develop Jumbo as a focused global entity.

11) Priya Paul: Priya Paul (born 1967), is a prominent woman entrepreneur of India, and currently the Chairperson of Appeejay the Park Hotels chain of boutique hotels. She joined the company, after finishing her studies in Economics at the Wellesley College (US) working under her father, as Marketing Manager at the Park Hotel, Delhi, at the age of 22.

After the death of Surrendra Paul, she succeeded him in 1990 as the Chairperson of the Hospitality Division of the Apeejay Surendra Group.

Her contributions to industry and commerce, particularly in the field of Hospitality Industry have been repeatedly recognized and she has received several awards and citations, including the following:

- The Federation of Hotels and Restaurants Association of India conferred on her Young Entrepreneur of the Year award (1999-2000),
- She was nominated for The Economic Times Awards as the Businessperson of the year (2002-2003), and
- UK's Tatler magazine rated The Park (Bangalore, India), a part of her Group, as one of the best Hotel Worldwide in 2003

12) Neelam Dhawan: Neelam Dhawan, Managing Director, Microsoft India, leads Microsoft India. She is a graduate from St. Stephens College in 1980, and also passed out from Delhi's Faculty of Management studies in 1982. Then she was keen on joining FMCG majors like Hindustan Lever and Asian Paints, both companies rejected Dhawan, as they did not wish to appoint women for marketing and sales.

13) Naina Lal Kidwai: Naina Lal Kidwai was the first Indian woman to graduate from Harvard Business School. Fortune magazine listed Kidwai among the world's top 50 Corporate Women from 2000 to 2003. According to the Economic times, she is the first woman to head the operations of a foreign bank in India. (HSBC)

14) Indu Jain: Indu Jain, the multi-faceted lady used to be the Chairman of the Times Group-The most powerful and largest Media house India has known. Indu Jain is known by many different identities such as that of spiritualist, humanist, entrepreneur, an educationalist but most prominently she played the role of the Chairman of Times Group. Indu Jain is the perfect picture of the successful Indian Woman entrepreneur.

15) Mallika Srinivasan: Mallika Srinivasan, currently the Director of TAFE-Tractors and Farm Equipment, India , was honoured with the title of Businesswoman of the Year during 2006 by the Economic Times. She joined the company in 1986 and has since been responsible for accelerating turnover from 85 crores to 2900 crores within a span of 2 decades.

16) Preetha Reddy: Preetha Reddy, Managing Director of Apollo Hospitals,

Chennai, one of the largest healthcare conglomerates of India, is one of the pioneer business women of India in the segment of Health Care Industry.

17) Ranjana Kumar: Ranjana Kumar, currently Vigilance Commissioner in Central Vigilance Commission, after her retirement as the Chairperson of NABARD- National Bank For Agricultural and Rural Development, is a prominent Indian Banker. When the Government of India appointed her as the Chairperson and Managing Director of The Indian Bank, she became the first woman to become head of a public sector bank in India. At that time of her appointment, The Indian Bank was saddled with huge losses and during her tenure she ensured the turnaround of The Indian Bank.

Women like these are an inspiration for all other women who strive to achieve great heights in their lives. Taking them as our role models each one of us can be there where they are right now. All we need have is faith in ourselves, confidence and above all a fixed aim that we need work towards.

Women Entrepreneurs may be defined as the women or group of women who initiate, organize and co-operate a business enterprise. Government of India has defined women entrepreneurs as an enterprise owned and controlled by a woman having a minimum financial interest of 51% of the capital and giving atleast 51% of employment generated in the enterprise to women.

The Indian women are no longer treated as show pieces to be kept at home. They are also enjoying the impact of globalization and making an influence not only on domestic but also on international sphere. Women are doing a wonderful job striking a balance between their house and career.

Conclusion

India is brimming with the success stories of women. They stand tall from the rest of the crowd and are applauded for their achievements in their respective field. These women leaders are assertive, persuasive and willing to take risks. They managed to survive and succeed in this cut throat competition with their hard work, diligence and perseverance.

Ability to learn quickly from her abilities, her persuasiveness, open style of problem solving, willingness to take risks and chances, ability to motivate people, knowing how to win and lose gracefully are the of the Indian women entrepreneurs.

In a recent survey it is revealed that the female entrepreneurs from India are generating more wealth than the women in any part of the world. The basic qualities required for entrepreneurs and the basic characters of Indian women, reveal that, much potential is available among the Indian women on their entrepreneurial ability. This potential is to be recognized, brought out and exposed for utilization in productive and service sectors for the development of the nation.

4

FEMALE ENTREPRENEUR

Female entrepreneurs, also known as **women entrepreneurs**, encompass approximately 1/3 of all entrepreneurs worldwide.

Demographic Characteristics

Studies have shown that successful Women entrepreneurs start their businesses as a second or third profession. Because of their previous careers, women entrepreneurs enter the business world later on in life, around 40–60 years old. As women are now overtaking their male peers when it comes to education, having higher education degrees is one of significant characteristics that many successful female entrepreneurs have in common.

International Implications

A recent international study found that women from low to middle income countries were more likely to enter early stage entrepreneurship when compared to those of higher income countries. A significant factor that may play a role in this disparity can be contributed to the fact that women from low income countries often seek an additional means of income to support themselves and their families. Overall, 40 to 50 per cent of all small businesses are owned by women in developing countries. Alternatively, this may also be due to the fact that, in western business practices, it is not seen as beneficial to exhibit feminine traits. While eastern businesses tend to follow methods based around mutual respect and understanding, western business expectations are for business leaders to be more ruthless, headstrong and less sensitive or respectful. "In the grab for power women use whatever means available to them, whereas a man would take a club to his opponents head a woman is more likely use other less forceful and more subversive measures. Let's just own it we have different weapons in our arsenal."

Present Challenges

Even though female entrepreneurship and the formation of women business networks is steadily rising, there are a number of challenges and obstacles that female entrepreneurs face. One major challenge that many women entrepreneurs may face is the traditional gender-roles society may still have on women. Entrepreneurship is still considered as a male-dominated field, and it may be difficult to surpass these conventional views. Other than dealing with the dominant stereotype, women entrepreneurs are facing several obstacles related to their businesses.

Obstacles Specific to Starting New Firms

External finance and sex discrimination

In general, women have lower personal financial assets than men. This means that for a given opportunity and equally capable individual, women must secure additional resources compared to men in order to exploit the opportunity because they control less capital. A question that has developed into its own sub-field in the women's entrepreneurship literature is if women have a harder time getting finance than men for the same business opportunity.

A specific solution for solving women's difficulties for obtaining financing has been micro financing. Micro finance is a financial institution that has become exceptionally popular especially in developing economies.

Obstacles specific to managing a small firm

Studies on women entrepreneurs show that women have to cope with stereotypic attitudes towards women on a daily basis. Business relations as customers, suppliers, banks, etc. constantly remind the entrepreneur that she is different, sometimes in a positive way such as by praising her for being a successful entrepreneur even though being a woman. Employees tend to mix the perceptions of the manager with their images of female role models leading to mixed expectations on the woman manager to be a manager as well as a "mother". The workload associated with being a small business manager is also not easily combined with taking care of children and a family. However, even if the revenues are somewhat smaller, women entrepreneurs feel more in control and happier with their situation than if they worked as an employee.

Bstacles specific to growing firms

A specific problem of women entrepreneurs seems to be their inability to achieve growth especially sales growth. [9] Another previously addressed issue is finance and as stated previously, the entrepreneurial process is somewhat dependent on initial conditions. In other words, as women often have a difficult time to assemble external resources, they start less ambitious firms that can be financed to a greater degree by their own available resources. This also has consequences for the future growth of the firm. Basically, firms with more resources at start-up have a higher probability to grow than firms with fewer resources. By resources is meant here societal position, human resources and financial resources. This initial endowment in the firm is therefore of great importance for firm survival and especially for firm growth. Despite that many women entrepreneurs face growth barriers; they are still able to achieve substantial firm growth. There are examples of that both in a number of developing economies (Ethiopia, Tanzania and Zambia) surveyed by the ILO, as well as in more developed economies such as the United States.

Encouragement of women entrepreneurs

In 1993, "Take Our Daughters to Work Day" was popularized to support career exploration for girls, later expanded to take Our Daughters and Sons to Work Day.

Female-only taxi companies in India, the UAE and Brazil support working women.

Women Entrepreneurs: A Critical Review of the Literature

Increasing numbers of women are becoming leaders of their own businesses, and many are struggling to achieve success. A growing body of theory and research is exploring how different women come to business ownership, their unique leadership challenges and strategies for success, their personal change and the processes of leadership development they experience. This paper reviews literature addressing women business owners from the general perspective of understanding their leadership. Within this frame, existing studies of women business owners are classified and examined according to four themes that appear to be most prominent. These four themes are

(1) Women business owners' characteristics and development;
(2) Women's motives for starting and leading a business;
(3) Women's leadership styles and management strategies in small business; and
(4) Barriers and conflicts encountered by women business owners.

Women Leaders in Small Business:

A Critical Review of Existing Literature and Questions for Future Inquiry

Women's leadership in contexts of small business ownership can be argued to present different models of leadership style, values, and challenges than those developed by women in organizational leadership roles. Recent studies of women in business ownership suggest that these women business owner-leaders exercise a large degree of control over the vision and purpose of the enterprise, and often deliberately craft working environments and cultures that support their personal values and preferences. They can cultivate their own working relationships with greater freedom. They can seek as much challenge and take as much risk as they can personally manage. For some women, these freedoms come at a high cost of fears and insecurities, unpredictable workload and isolation. In sum, small business ownership creates leadership issues for women that are different in kind than those shared by their sisters in senior management positions located in corporate or government settings.

In the 1990's across North America, women increasingly have been entering ventures in self-employment. In the USA, by 1992 women already owned 27 percent of small businesses. In Canada, this figure in 1996 was 40 percent. Statistics collected in 1997-98 found that women were starting businesses in North America at two to five times the rate of men and that increasing numbers of these were home-based. There is also evidence of a trend of women in senior management leaving or wanting to leave their corporate positions to try business ownership. In the U.S. from 1987-99, women's businesses increased 103%, their sales grew 436% and their employee ranks swelled 320%. Various estimates claim that by the year 2000, almost 50 percent of all new businesses in North America will have been started by women. World-wide, similar patterns are becoming evident. Women-owned businesses are increasing to comprise one-quarter to one-third of businesses in the formal economies of Brazil, Equador, Mexico, Australia, Ireland, Italy, England, Germany, France, and certain African countries, and women business owners of these countries share similar concerns, according to surveys conducted 1997-98 at international conferences by the National Foundation of Women Business Owners.

A growing body of literature is emerging to study the phenomenon of women's leadership as small business owners along a wide variety of dimensions, drawing from perspectives ranging from market models of business economic development to women's psychological development and feminist studies of women's leadership. Qualitative studies in the past five years have indicated contested issues related to values, identity and the meaning of leadership emerging in this trend of women business ownership. Women don't always accept the dominant formula that success equals money and power. Women who start their own business sometimes do so to craft a new way of working, and many continue to fight barriers related to traditional constructs of economic power and expectations. Many women business owners claim that the whole experience changes them profoundly.

The purpose of this paper is first to provide a critical overview of selected literature exploring women's small business ownership, and second to pose questions arising from the existing literature to guide further research and theorizing about women's leadership in small business contexts. In her 1992 review of existing literature, Brush concluded that women's business leadership cannot be understood using traditional frameworks of business analysis. She writes, "Significant differences have been found in reasons for business start-up, educational background, work experience and business skills business goals, management styles, business characteristics and growth rates. These variations suggest that women perceive and approach business differently than men." Research related to women's leadership in business ownership has produced findings and theory that can be divided into four general themes outlined briefly below. These themes were selected for discussion because of their prevalence in literature of the past two decades addressing women's business ownership, much of it published in recognized journals of small business management.

This is to argue here that there are two main difficulties with some of this literature. First, comparisons of women to men business owners continue to be prevalent in business ownership literature. Gender-comparative studies have focused on psychological characteristics such as propensity to take risks, leadership dimensions such as levels of experience and education, and networking styles. The problem lies in the legacy of this comparative approach: many constructs applied to analyse women's small business leadership approaches and needs continue to be derived from male orientations. Feminist writers such as Hart have shown the limitations and incongruence of male leadership patterns applied to women's experiences. Meanwhile in small business literature women are sometimes portrayed as deficit, requiring training to compete with traditional business models measuring success according to profit, growth and size.

Second, much of this literature continues to rely upon assumptions grounded in individualist psychology. Attributes of women business owners are often presumed inherent, and leadership styles are sometimes generalized as if there existed "women's ways" of leading. Also neglected is specific attention to relationships between the emergence of women's leadership in small business, and the changing cultural and political-economic dynamics of the marketplace. What may be helpful is a more critical analysis of the discourses within which different women in particular cultural-economic contexts are construing their meanings of leadership and success and the possibilities available to them. Finally, the nature of gendered work and barriers in both leadership and business ownership need to be analysed within these frameworks.

The four themes are briefly introduced in the following paragraphs. Within each theme, more recent literature is expanding the scope of issues being explored and the depth and richness of the exploration. These themes are discussed in detail in later sections.

Women business owners' psychological characteristics were a focus of many early studies; showing the historical interest in relationships between psychological profile and leadership success. More recently, studies of women's personal development and change related to their small business leadership experiences is a recurring theme. These tend to highlight the importance of women's struggles with identity and personal change in leading their own business, including shaping their own role in the venture.

Women's motives for starting and leading a business have been documented in many studies to help illuminate the desires and needs of women leaders who choose business ownership over organizational management positions. Women's reasons for business start-up reasons encompass a wide range: desiring greater work-life flexibility, seeking challenge, fulfilling a long-felt desire, or escaping an organizational glass ceiling.

Women's leadership styles and approaches have become prominent in studies situated in larger organizations. However in small business literature, the focus tends to be women's business management strategies rather than their visions, values, and relational processes. Management strategies often tend to be reported from statistical studies grounded in market models which examine women's business growth rates, business planning ability, and possession of management training against traditional expectations of small business management. While a few have drawn attention to the possibility that women's leadership approaches in small business are unique, there is still little substantial research exploring this area. Value choices in leadership of women entrepreneurs, including women entrepreneurs' meanings of success and values respecting work, money, and family, is a theme emerging in some recent writings on women entrepreneurs that embraces many tensions and dilemmas.

Barriers and conflicts encountered by women business owners are sometimes studied from a feminist perspective which critiques the structural and ideological discrimination built in to the existing economy and tacitly-agreed western models of business growth. Reports include isolation and gender-based discrimination of various kinds, exclusion from male networks, and limited access to capital. Work-family conflict experienced by women business owners has been a focus of recent studies.

These four themes will be discussed in more detail in the following sections, and suggested directions for further inquiry will be posed at the conclusion of the paper. This review is intended to be representative, not comprehensive. Any categorization like this one makes compromises to produce certain clarity. Such a broad review may blur important internal differences within each perspective, and build the illusion of static reification of these dynamic themes. Hopefully these limitations may be overlooked in face of the potential usefulness of this review. The overall intention of the article is to outline scholarly understandings of women's entrepreneurial leadership that are accumulating in the four themes outlined here, to challenge certain apparent limitations in existing research, and to present questions for further study of women's leadership as small business owners.

As the following paragraphs should make clear, women's experiences as owner-leaders are not unitary, nor should women business-owners be treated as a monolithic group in some sort of misguided search for 'women's ways' of doing business. A critical theme threaded throughout this discussion is the need to resist any urge to homogenize women into clear patterns, and to emphasize their differentiated opportunities, approaches, and perceptions of leadership.

Women business owners' characteristics and development

Studies of business-owners' characteristics continue to compare women to men. Most studies have concluded that women are more similar to men business owners than they are different, in terms of both psychological and demographic characteristics. Marital status, age (30-45), birth order and having a self-employed father are characteristics reported to be similar across men and women business owners. General personal characteristics of so-called successful women business owners identified through survey research include autonomy, persistence, hard work, competitiveness, orientation to personal achievement and higher income, belief in one's own vision, goal-setting, risk-taking, and natural leadership qualities.

Caruana, Morris, and Vella, in their study of Maltese export firms, found that women and men business owners show similarity in demonstrating three characteristics deemed key for business owners: innovativeness; risk-taking; and proactiveness. Masters and Meier found women's entrepreneurial risk-taking to be almost as high as men's, although they did not consider respondents' personal meanings of what constitutes risk in a particular situation. Sexton and Bowman-Upton found that in comparison to men, women have higher willingness to accept change and greater need for autonomy while having lower energy levels and risk-taking propensities.

Now, we have the first problem with such studies of 'characteristics' is their assumption that observable behaviours emanate from inner traits. This psychological view has been challenged by critical cultural writings of the past two decades which claim that people's so-called 'characteristics' are in fact produced within a web of cultural practices, social interactions, images and language. Second, such studies appear to be motivated by a fundamental belief that personal traits are significantly linked to organizational development and success in a cause-effect relationship. However, critics of leadership trait theory have shown the weaknesses in this link, arguing that leadership is enacted in socially constructed contexts and cannot be attributed to inherent characteristics. Third, these characteristics are all reported as broad dimensions in isolation, lacking situatedness in particular local histories, and cultural and socio-political contexts which women business owners must confront. These psychological dimensions unfortunately present a static, cookie-cutter model which implies an entrepreneur is born, not developed and continually developing. Chell questions whether the "heffalump" of entrepreneurism actually exists, arguing that entrepreneurs present different characteristics in different lights at different times. From gender perspectives, an essentializing approach tends to contribute to assumptions that a unitary set of 'women's ways' of doing business can be identified. This not only obscures important distinctions and inequities, but leads to unfortunate assertions of "womanliness accessing femininity" offering new hope for corporatism with kindness and gentleness.

Fourth, several of these business owner 'characteristics' studies, in comparing women to men, fail to attend to individual women's needs, development, meanings, and changing responses to their contexts. Many feminist writers argue that approaches and descriptors suitable for exploring women's experience are incommensurate with those that might be useful for analyzing men's patterns. For example, MacKeracher observes that women's 'self' is not single and solitary but woven into relational networks, and Clark and Dirkx argue that 'multiple' selves emerge and shift according to circumstance. Research and theory of women's development consistently report that their workplace learning is significantly rooted in self and relationships. Identity and intimacy appear to be central issues throughout women's lives, and women tend to develop their self-concept in a way that is intimately linked to their interactive relational connections with other people. In her comprehensive review of literature describing women entrepreneurs, Brush argues strongly for a new model through which to view and understand women business owners, one which recognizes that women view their business as a network of relationships in which the changing self is woven.

Some researchers have called attention to the wide variation in women business owners' characteristics and approaches to their business. Robertson provides case studies of diverse women who started a business through financial need or personal change, rather than because of desire for achievement or personal vision. Some worked more collaboratively than competitively, sought relational more than autonomal ways of working, and were oriented more to service and contribution than to higher-income goals. Gay's narratives illustrate women business owners developing certain characteristics according to the circumstances of their history and the nature of business challenges they experience. 'Characteristics' are contradictory: some women describe their low self-esteem, tendencies to personalize relationships and shoulder others' problems along with challenge-seeking, proactive aggression. In any case, the whole area of women's development has grown to contribute more differentiated, dynamic models from which women leadership as business owners can be better understood. Yet as Chell argues, a stereotypic view of 'individualism, aggressive competitiveness and self-interest', while inaccurate, somehow continues to be reproduced.

Meanwhile, feminist poststructural perspectives advanced by writers such as Lather, Orner, and Tisdell have called for analysis of the ways women's subjectivity is produced through cultural discourses. Thus the characteristics of human subjectivity emerge through engagement within the practices, discourses, moralities and institutions that lend significance to the events in their worlds. Lather explains that through discursive struggle for subjectivities people occupy conflicting subject positions, some received and others created, marked by contradictory meanings and pleasures. Especially in an age of semiotic glut, humans are "constantly figured and refigured within a context of bombardment by conflicting messages. This feminist poststructural frame encourages discursive analysis of how subjectivities are regulated through positionality, knowledge construction, voice, and authority, and makes gender prominent in the analysis. As Tisdell explains, "the connections between one's individual identity and social structures" are the focus in poststructural feminism. This conceptual view holds promise for reframing what formerly have been accepted as women business owners' innate characteristics, and analyzing women's negotiations as owner-leaders in business start-up and development among the discursive meanings and practices swirling around them. One study has examined how women business-owners and these contradictory discourses inform and shape one another.

Women's motives for starting and leading a business

Studies of reasons given by women for starting their own business have been prominent especially in the early studies of female entrepreneurship; claim Carter and Cannon, although few studies developed sophisticated taxonomies. Women's start-up motives may be particularly instructive in understanding women's leadership needs and preferences. Among the reasons, workplace dissatisfaction seems significant: much literature has documented women's struggles with what they perceive to be inflexible workplace structures and expectations, incompatible communication styles, and ethical conflicts. From a feminist perspective Hart, among others, argues that many workplaces provide a miseducative context for women. She claims that women seek environments where they may find communality, validate their subjectivity, engage concretely in work that matters, and root their work in reciprocal, caring networks.

The Business Development Bank found significant differences between men's and women's business goals: for men, financial gain is a primary objective. Although there are variations, many women emphasize that their primary goals in starting a business are not financial. So why would women give up income security, job status and stability for the high risk, hard work and often low income of business ownership? One dominant motive reported by women surveyed in past studies was to create greater flexibility for balancing work and family. In more recent studies women continue to emphasize flexibility as a primary motivator for business start-up, along with other personal reasons: need for more challenge, independence, passion for a particular idea, and desire for greater fulfillment and meaning in their work. Women also represent the fastest-growing group of home-based business-owners, entering five times more than men. Reasons appear to include low start-up costs, a perceived significant increase in personal productivity working at home, and the fact that personal skills that may not be marketable to an outside company can be used to start a business from home.

Self-actualization is the most important reason given by women in a survey of 223 business owners, including goals of maximizing personal skills/abilities, contributing to society, and gaining respect and recognition. Interestingly, this study also found that women who have lost their jobs through 'restructuring' tend more than men to turn to self-employment instead of pounding the pavement in search of another job. In Gay's interview study, women business owners stated frequently their desire to prove "I can do it'". Fasci and Valdez found business ownership attracts women accountants as a viable avenue to achieve career success, gain control of their destiny and the respect of their peers, create their own work environments, and ensure their advancement is truly based on merit -- all dimensions that women perceive to be less available to them when employed in someone else's enterprise.

Many women business owners quit leadership positions in larger organizations, a theme supporting the possibility of systemic organizational power imbalances and perhaps gendered corporate cultures. Sharp and sharp reported that of 165 executive women surveyed, 37% indicated strong possibility of leaving their job to start their own businesses. Reasons given by women leaders include feeling undervalued, experiencing little challenge and career development opportunity, and believing their contributions to be insufficiently acknowledged. The National Foundation of Women Business Owners found that fully half of women surveyed left a previous position primarily looking for more flexibility, but also describing a desire to "follow an entrepreneurial dream", a need for greater challenge in their work, and "glass ceiling" issues such as gendered limitations in opportunity and creative freedom . Catalyst confirmed this trend and reported similar reasons. Other recent studies such as Baridon and Eyler document women's frustration with glass ceiling issues that continues to prevent their promotion in many organizations. Ferguson and Durup had reported that women starting their own business to escape perceived gendered conditions contributing to their underemployment, work-related stress, and difficulties managing work-family balance.

These reasons continue to be echoed in research focusing on women business owners. Moore and Buttner, in their comprehensive U.S. study surveying and interviewing 129 women entrepreneurs, followed with focus groups one year later, ask the question, "Why and how did women with exposure to corporate life decide first to enter the organization and then to leave it for entrepreneurship?". Their findings revealed five thematic clusters of reasons women left their jobs to start a business: need for self-determination and challenge; blocks to corporate advancement; organizational dynamics that dealt with power and politics; and desire for greater family-career balance.

The Lee and Rogoff study concluded that women's goals for business start-up were similar to men's: for example, almost half of women and men surveyed chose the following statement from seven alternatives: "Creating a new product or service had always been my dream". However, it is noteworthy that the other statements contained no references to creating flexibility for home/family, career dissatisfaction, controlling one's destiny and escaping gender discrimination, or any of the other reasons cited by women business owners. Moore and Buttner's conclusion is that despite some overlap, "other reasons appear special to women Gender, only occasionally in the form of discrimination, makes a difference".

Business start-up is not simply about goals, but also about process. Albert indicates that women experience phases of psychological crisis, "black hole", and personal transformation during the transition period from employment to self-employment, a phenomenon deserving attention from policy-makers and program planners determining women's support needs. Yaccato and Jubinville compare women's processes of starting a business to pregnancy, birth, and child-rearing, explaining that business start-up for women is a very personal endeavor of nurturing a private dream, entwined with issues of identity and personal relationship.

Business starts of women must be assessed in terms of particular contexts and conditions. Their motives and approaches must be examined carefully against their own goals and standards. Although there are continuing calls for further studies comparing women to men business owners, a serious question needs to be raised relative to conclusions such as those reported in the Lee and Rogoff study. As Moore and Buttner assert, research still tends to measure women according to traditional models of business ownership created by the men who dominated business-ownership in North America until the past fifteen years. We need to ask why there is a perceived need to compare women to men business owners, and whether such comparison is appropriate.

Women's start-up motives and enterprise goals are unique. Their reasons for entering business appear to depend partly on 'push' factors such as gendered discrimination they encounter in jobs, and partly on 'pull' factors such as seeking greater fulfillment, accomplishment and control in their work. All of these dimensions appear to vary according to different women's positionality in terms of socio-economic condition, race, geographic location, former education, experience and community of networks. Careful research probing relationships among these dimensions would be helpful for three reasons. First, it may help illuminate the difficulties that potential women leaders encounter in existing workplace organizations and perhaps suggest changes to work conditions that might keep women from leaving. Second, careful analysis of their objectives may help trace the contours of alternate models of enterprise development emerging under the leadership of at least some women. Finally, understanding those desires drawing increasing numbers of different women into leadership as small business owners may open spaces for analysing the changing nature of work and of women's expectations and needs related to work, in an increasing technologized, globalized economy.

Women's leadership styles and management strategies in small business

Women's small business leadership has been frequently compared with men's. Some claim that women's and men's business management skills appear not to vary significantly. Others, however, claim that women business-owners tend to lack management skills, training or experience, and good business plans. Other studies have questioned dominant views of what counts as "good" business skills, arguing that conventional 'male-oriented' premises may distort the ways women in business are judged. Studies have noted women's tendency not to expand their business and increase profits, their unique focus on personal and social goals as well as economic goals stressed by male-owned businesses, their tendency to initiate service-oriented businesses and sole proprietorships, their lack of previous experience in executive management or entrepreneurism, and their access to fewer role models than men. As Brush and later Moore and Buttner conclude, such findings indicate that women have different goals and develop different processes of business decision-making, planning, and structuring than men.

The leadership style of women business owners has received attention in various studies showing parallels to studies of women's executive leadership in corporations. Management studies have declared that women attend more to process than to "bottom line": they are concerned with how their actions affect others; appreciate diversity, and stress teamwork and the interpersonal. Women leaders supposedly tend to emphasize democratic participation by all, using multi-directional "power-with" authority to energize others to actively participate. Women leaders have also been characterized as showing passionate commitment to collective action and to change.

Similar patterns appear in studies of women's leadership as small business owners. Wells shows women business owners to be highly motivated by community needs, and to favor collaborative management approaches. Another recent US study asserts that women-owned companies are more likely to be "family friendly", offering flextime and job-sharing benefits. Moore and Buttner identify among women entrepreneurs an "interactive" leadership style that integrates transformational, role model/visionary, and web approaches to leadership. The interactive style demonstrates greater concern for staff welfare; pays less attention to formal power and more to personal power; and believes in the importance of empowering staff.

However in small business ownership, women leaders must balance many roles: strategic planner, accountant, marketer, product developer, human resource manager, to name a few. As Brush points out, Moore and Buttner's emphasis on the effectiveness of transformational leadership is not clearly operationalized or measured. Desires to nurture staff often conflict with needs to please customers and survive, according to the findings of Godfrey, Robertson, and Thrasher and Smid. Leadership oriented to a vision of collaboration must somehow be reconciled with issues of authority, control, and competitiveness, forcing many women business owners to navigate between competing values and expectations.

The importance of values and women business owners' struggles with them are clearly entwined with their choices and changes as owner-leaders of small business. A few studies have examined this area, usually treating 'values' as something possessed, substantive and inherent, and examining how an owner's identifiable 'value' affects her leadership. Olson and Currie for example found that women entrepreneurs' values, infusing their management strategies, were influenced by whether their industry was male-dominated or not. Good and Mistick suggest there exist misconceptions about women's business intents and decision-making, and claim that these must be interpreted within a clearer understanding of women's unique value systems.

More recently, some studies are exploring women leaders' 'values' as a dynamic site of contradiction and even struggle. Three patterns related to the values of entrepreneurial women indicate sources of tension which these women must confront. The first is related to leadership style: women leaders often try to balance caring for the welfare of individuals with concern for justice and conflicting individual rights, and face dilemmas when their vision of collaborative community conflict with multiple power dynamics, differing values and agendas.

A second source of tension for women owner-leaders is related to meanings of success. Soldressen, Fiorito, and He draw attention to the inadequacy of traditional measures of business success based on financial performance and expansion, and personal success based on achieving material wealth, for describing women. Studies have reported that many women view success as achieving balance of work and family, self-fulfillment and helping others, or working at something they love, despite what may be low income. Fenwick and Hutton report, in a study interviewing 110 Canadian women owners of small business, those women emphasized the secondary importance of money and material goods in their lives. They tended to describe their work success as building mutually supportive relationships among their staff and networks of suppliers and competitors, making qualitative contributions to their communities, creating reputations as reliable and effective, and sustaining 'quality of life' for themselves, their families and the people connected with their enterprise. Quality of life was more typically represented by examples of 'right relationship' than by material markers. Moore and Buttner found that self-fulfillment was the most important measure of success for women heading small firms: "Success seems to be measured internally in terms of personal growth, professional development, and improving one's skills, rather than measured externally in profits or business growth. Money, then, is a means and not an end". However, it can be speculated that the micro-practices of balancing such values with business demands amidst the profit discourse and competitive pressures of a globalized marker might be complex.

A third tension for some women is connected with business planning. Writing a business plan is a conventional starting point for conceiving the terms and constraints of one's practice in running a business, according to pre-determined constructs, to obtain start-up capital from financial institutions. A good business plan guarantees a degree of credibility for the new business-owner, signifying proper preparation, organization, and goal-setting according to logics of prediction and control.

Thus a business planning discourse disciplines and regulates enterprise creators through their own desires to be taken seriously and granted venture capital, in telephone interviews of 9,553 Norwegian women entrepreneurs, found that women were far less likely than men to prepare a business plan. They suggest therefore that even though the lack of business plans did not result in lower business success, that initiatives should encourage women to write such plans. North American women also have been targeted for training in business planning as one outcome of many 1980s studies concluding that women had less formal business education and experience than men, and needed to improve their competitive potential. Embedded in this logic is a shared and unproblematic acceptance of a 'right way' to do business, an efficiency ethic, and a will to suppress alternate approaches in sustaining the dominant. However, Fenwick and Hutton show that for some, the prediction-and-control logic based on principles of competition and autonomy of the traditional business plan is counter-productive. Fenwick and Hutton claim that some women entrepreneurs are experimenting with more emergent, fluid, intuitive ways of developing an enterprise vision and plan, although such non-conventional approaches invite skepticism and even attack from the business community.

Vision can be argued to be another key dimension of enterprise leadership, strategy implementation and change; vision both embeds values and ensures the success of an enterprise. Falbe and Larwood found significant differences between the vision of entrepreneurs and non-entrepreneurs in terms of action-oriented flexibility, and envisioning the organization as an extension of themselves and their needs. Some studies of women business owners have also found their vision to be linked closely to self-expression. In a recent qualitative study of Texan women business owners, Wells found identity to be central in women's business visions and sense of achievement, and their learning about self through business ownership to influence their leadership strategy in terms of changing business goals, staff management, and planning focus. Albert documents women's attempts to break away from traditional definitions of career and job roles that limit their growth or fragment their lives, to invent work allowing them to integrate various parts of self. Like Albert, Brook argues that many North American women in mid-life are grappling with identity issues which often lead them to 'quit' traditional employment. Stories of women business owners indicate that deep needs to express self meaningfully through work and to make a contribution to the world often lead to business start-up, and that profound personal change is often experienced throughout the process of business development.

Barriers and conflicts encountered by women business owners

Research has established the smaller size, dramatically lower profits and take-home pay of women's businesses compared to men's. One study of women's businesses reported general "disappointment" that women business owners face the same sort of pay gap as salaried female workers, possibly related to the type of businesses women initiate, their reported difficulties in securing bank financing, women's business skills, and the lower fees-for-service women are able to command. These issues must be interpreted carefully. When using different frames of analysis what appear to be 'barriers' may be deliberate choice, and what appear to be naturalized conditions may be structural but invisible inequities.

Within feminist frames, gendered work structures create broad barriers that pervade social and economic relations in which women owner-leaders practice. Probert synthesizes feminist research on women's work to show many themes relevant to this discussion:

1. gendered division of work: hierarchies of skill reflect a 'male dominance in craft identity' and sustain a distinction between men's and women's work;
2. subsequent to (1), pervasive undervaluing of women's skills and services;
3. gendered division of family responsibilities affecting women's overall workload, patterns of work participation and perceptions of them as less committed;
4. gendered opportunities restricting women's access to leadership training and positions of authority;
5. increasing casualization of the workforce throwing many women into self-employment; and
6. Continued low pay, low status and low opportunity in feminized industries such as retailing and banking.

For women business-owners, these inequities can be argued to be implicated in women's decision to start a business, the kind and scope of business they undertake and its perceived credibility and profitability, their attempts to seek funding and establish commercial networks, and, for some, their lack of leadership experience and training prior to becoming an owner-leader. However, the literature offers conflicting ways of viewing and responding to these issues. As Barrett explains, liberal feminism recommends lifting the barriers to ensure women business owners' full participation in the market, while social feminists argue that 'women's ways' as business owners need to be celebrated in their own right. Liberal feminism doesn't question the system but fiddles with details that improve the lives of some women, particularly the upwardly mobile. Feminist poststructuralists would argue against any unitary treatment of women, and perhaps suggest that 'barriers' might be better analyzed as systemic power relations in which different women negotiate positionality, identity and voice by virtue of their particular culture, class, age, and authority.

Some studies in the 1980's began to report unique barriers confronting women business owners. There is most significant for business viability included discrimination experienced by women seeking venture capital and exclusion from financial business networks. In the 1990's women business owners apparently continued to confront significant gender-related obstacles including limited access to capital, difficulty in competing for government contracts, and lack of information about where to get assistance. Women reported that they had to work harder to prove their competence to suppliers and clients, and to be taken seriously. Others often underestimated women's ability to start a venture and discouraged them from "dreaming big". Women still report struggling with others' diminishment of the significance of their enterprise: the "little business" syndrome. However, despite their stories of gender discrimination, many individual women interviewed. Gay and Robertson claim that their obstacles are simply the challenges of small business shared by all business owners. Evidently this area requires further study.

A primary and continuing obstacle faced by women appears to be difficulty in securing capital funding for new business ventures. Riding and Swift concluded financial conditions for women business owners were less favorable than for men: women more often had to pay higher interest rates, find more collateral, and provide a spouse's co-signature. Strauss claims that by 1994-95 in North America, statistics made it clear that women were starting 40% of businesses and were still receiving only 3-4% of venture capital funds. However Buttner counters that some women have been unprepared with the comprehensive business plan demanded by the banks: rather than do their homework they attributed their loan difficulties to gender discrimination. Yet women interviewed in qualitative studies tell stories about their business plans being scrutinized more carefully and having to meet more special demands than men's; Robertson. There are signs that the financial situation is changing: recent studies indicate that women now have more access to capital, as certain financial institutions and government loan programs have specifically targeted needs of women business-owners; Bank of Montreal. And as Strauss points out, in the New Economy women of all ages are starting dotcom businesses which do not require much venture capital. Further study is needed to clarify this issue from different perspectives.

However, more attention perhaps should be paid also to the subtle ways women's choices are regulated by the pervasive cultural emphases placed on competition, profit, and growth. Many discursive and material practices patrol the boundaries between women business owners and the networks leading to venture capital. Carter and Kolvereid, comparing differences between new women and men entrepreneurs in the U.S. and Norway found that women had smaller financial resources than men, came from households with lower incomes: almost 60% of the men successfully started the business compared to only 24% of the women. Critics who attribute women's failure to obtain necessary funds for start-up to their lack of a proper business plan reinforce the tightly circumscribed discourse of a 'right' way to do business. This militates against the alternate approaches that some women experiment with. Meanwhile Thrasher and Smid argue that many women business-owners tend to undervalue their own work, echoing Godfrey's claim that certain women are complicit in a gendered diminishment of their enterprise. Thus they are less assertive about seeking financing and undercharge for their services. Thrasher and Smid suggest that this discursive dynamic ultimately results in women business-owners accepting a reduced quality of life because of their ambivalence about money.

Another significant barrier for some owner-leaders reported in the literature has been networking. Studies a decade old showed that few men business owners included women in their close business networks. Women business owners were often traditionally excluded from "old boy networks", were perceived to have more "affective" and less "instrumental" motives in building relationships, and relied more on spouses for information and support than on outside advisors such as bankers and lawyers. Networks of contacts, important to both men and women business owners, differed in content and size. Women's networks tended to be composed of women and were smaller than men's networks, which may be one reason for certain difficulties reported by women in obtaining financing. Women were seeking special women's networks, and women tended to rely on their networks not only for information but also for personal support. A study of Canadian women business owners concluded that they worked in a "glass box": isolated by overload, they had not the necessary time to cultivate or use important support networks.

However, a more recent study of networking has concluded that women are as active as men entrepreneurs in networking to obtain assistance, and as successful as men in obtaining high-quality assistance including resources. By contrast, Moore and Buttner conclude that women use networks primarily for sounding boards rather than resource acquisition. One problem here is the lack of contextualization in findings. How women create and use networks could reasonably by presumed to be connected with both their environments and their business size, nature, and purpose. Sawyerr and McGee found significant differences between personal networks of new firm owner/managers and those of more mature firms, and show strong relationships between environmental uncertainty and networking activity and intensity. Chell has shown the importance of analysing relationships between personal networks and labor market inequalities to better understand how which individuals develop aspirations, access resources and build support for an enterprise. Brush suggests that network uses rely on business needs, which vary according to size, scope and sector. Thus research exploring the function of networks in business leadership should be carefully situated, and compare links between relational dynamics, individual needs and values, leadership approaches and outcomes in terms of business success as women owner' leaders define it.

A third key struggle for women business owners are related to balancing family issues. Work-family conflict results from inter-role conflict caused by incompatible or conflicting pressures from work and family domains, including job-family role strain, work-family interference, and work-nonwork role conflict. Women are more likely to have primary domestic responsibility and to have interrupted careers, which create work-family conflict. Seeking balance in work-family has been established as a significant factor in women's decision to start a business, although women business owners still appear to experience much greater conflict than men in managing family and work life.

As discussed throughout this article, research throughout the past few decades has suggested that women start a business to create greater flexibility in their lives, to seek greater quality of life and more creative, meaningful work, and to place higher priority on relationships and family. If this is so, it puts certain women in tension with a highly competitive profit-driven marketplace, and presents a fundamental shift in the meaning of work and career for some women. Meanwhile, some studies show women business owners in inner turmoil, stretched between round-the-clock working hours and the great feelings of satisfaction and competence from their business, while suffering guilt and fragmentation while juggling family issues;. Sadly given these important issues, Ferguson and Durup show that specific study of work-family conflict experienced by women business owners is virtually non-existent.

Considerations for Future Research

Historically, the focus of research studying women entrepreneurs tended towards two main directions:

(1) a-historical, a-contextual, a-political description of women's businesses and ownership characteristics; and

(2) Comparison to men's businesses using economic measures derived from traditional male models.

A surprisingly extensive number of studies continue to measure women against men owner-leaders according to management style, goals, type of business, and approaches to planning and developing the business. Brush charges that the constructs, principles and language of business ownership governing the perspectives and questions of researchers have mostly been derived from "men's view of reality, based in autonomy, logic, and rule-based decision-making". Accordingly, some studies concluded that women fall short of the success achieved by their men colleagues in terms of management skills, business size, growth rate, and overall profits. Then a wave of studies in the 1990's, reviewed in the preceding paragraphs, examined women business owners' motives for start-up, leadership styles, and barriers. Though helpful in building initial understandings of diverse women business owners and detecting issues for policy and program attention, this research has sometimes been limited by its lack of attention to specific contexts and women's differentiated approaches and experiences. Also lacking in much of this research is consideration of gendered structures from a feminist perspective. Finally, there is a paucity of cultural analysis examining the production of women business owners' choices, experiences, meanings and values in prevailing discourses and practices of a globalized market and post-Fordist work environments.

Recent case studies and surveys of women business owners have explored some of these issues. These offer rich stories and analyse the transitions experienced by women starting businesses in various contexts and stages of life. A few qualitative research studies shed light on women's learning processes in business ownership. Some of these studies show the significance of women's lifelong learning, search for meaningful vocation and ecological living, identity formation, and transformation, in business start-up motives, leadership approaches, and business goals and structures which partially determine unique characteristics of women-owned businesses. There is indication that women are increasingly seeking to transform their lives by integrating their work, learning, personal life, and relationships in the venture they build. If so, women are generating new models for creating work and doing business which deserve continuing study by small business researchers. In the process, as Moore and Buttner demonstrate, women are experiencing significant personal change and developing distinctive models of leadership.

Meanwhile Barrett, drawing from Chell's questions about this 'heffalump' that is entrepreneurism, suggests that past efforts to examine entrepreneurism in its own right, divorced from analysing relationships with industry and gendered notions of work, may have been misguided. Barrett calls for future research using a variety of disciplines and research techniques to explore women in business. Carter and Cannon claim that theoretical frameworks are lacking. They urge future research that draws from sociological frames and debates, and combines more qualitative methods with quantitative. Chell goes further, stating "What is needed is a multi-paradigmatic approach in which local economic conditions and institutional frameworks can be described initially, with follow up investigative work assuming interpretivist/radical structural paradigms", to examine threads of local culture, socio-economy, gender and power.

The point is that future analysis of women's leadership in small business contexts would be well-served with more qualitative research, employing in-depth approaches such as life history, narrative inquiry, heuristic inquiry, discursive analysis and ethnography to balance the large-scale survey studies that have dominated examination of women entrepreneurs in the past two decades. Further, theoretical perspectives governing research needs to be expanded to include critical cultural studies, political economy, psychological development, and post-structuralism as well as different feminisms. These different lenses may help to decenter the predominant focus on women as isolated and somewhat exoticized actors, and help illuminate important relationships of women business owners' choices within changing social webs of action, meaning, knowledge and power to which Chell refers. Theoretical perspectives that deconstruct systemic power imbalances embedded in dominant business practices and models might help avoid potential feminization of the struggling micro-enterprise, where unreasonably long hours, low income and isolation do not support the triumphalist claims by writers such as O'Brien of women liberating themselves and their national economies through entrepreneurism. Ferguson argues feminist perspectives help move beyond the efficiency and effectiveness of business practices to question "the moral and political legitimacy of these practices: not how best to use the power that business accords certain groups of people but why these people are thus empowered".

Within these new perspectives and methodological approaches, questions for future research can be derived from various threads currently stirring amidst the four themes of research discussed in this article. Here are some examples:

- How do different women business-owners today understand and measure 'successes for their enterprise and their leadership? How are their values and meanings of success related to different women's unique models of business development?
- To what extent and for what specific reasons are women leaders in senior management turning to business ownership

as a result of general career dissatisfaction? What personal needs of women are met through owning a business that they perceive cannot be met through employment? What implications might this have for supporting women in business ownership?

- What are the relationships between women business owners' business start-up and development and the different personal, social and economic contexts in which they work? What contextual elements and personal dimensions have the greatest influence on different women's capacity to achieve success as they define it?
- How do entrepreneurial women view their changing self, and the relationships between their personal development and their choices regarding business development? What issues of identity, if any, do women business owners struggle with through the process of developing a business?
- What are the unique leadership approaches and challenges of women business owners in different stages of developing a business in different socio-economic-geographical contexts?
- What work/family conflicts do women business owners find significant, and at what points in business start-up and development are these greatest? How do various women developing different businesses perceive and manage these conflicts?
- What do women business owners now perceive to be the most significant obstacles to their success, as they define it, in changing contexts? To what extent are such obstacles related to gendered work and family issues?
- What information, resources, relationships, education, and other supports do different women business owners say have helped those most to meet challenges and achieve success as they define it?

Such questions move beyond essentialist ways of conceiving women business owners, help address complex dimensions of power and social context, eschew tendencies to examine women's business in terms of men's motives and strategies, and widen the vocabulary defining 'success' to embrace different women's own meanings and objectives. These questions also contribute to the four themes adopted by the 2000 OECD conference on women entrepreneurs in small and medium enterprise, which focus on improving knowledge about female entrepreneurship and its obstacles, fostering entrepreneurial culture and developing women-owned businesses.

Conclusion

This article has reviewed research about women's entrepreneurial leadership organized in four themes prominent in the existing literature: characteristics, reasons for business start-up, leadership approaches, and barriers Some of this literature homogenizes women, or reduces their complexity to simple models. Some is guided by constructs and language derived from models of men's business ownership which, as Lee and Rogoff point out, is in danger of producing policies and programs aiming to make women more like men business owners.

But together these four themes help move us toward important questions about women's leadership development in entrepreneurial contexts. How are different women transforming small business leadership in ways that may challenge traditional understandings of work, learning, career, and success? What personal needs do women meet through leading their own businesses? What kinds of knowledge do they value, and how do they develop this knowledge while growing a business? How are women's choices shaped by and shaping the changing dynamics and cultural discourses of their local socio-economic contexts?

The main intention of this article is to join the calls put forth by others for research attention to these and other complex questions. Women leading their own businesses are increasing, and have become the largest employer of the U.S. labor force. Meanwhile rapidly changing contexts and dynamics of work have shifted the demands of organizational leadership and the opportunities for alternate expressions of leadership. Women leaving jobs, particularly senior management ranks, to start businesses may be exemplifying Edwards' vision of 'post-Fordist artisans' that resist the oppressive structures and discourses of Taylorist workplaces: "active, creative, reflexive, risk-taking workers with certain degrees of autonomy in how they define and achieve their work goals, engaging in practices of social entrepreneurship".

Growing evidence asserts that women's entrepreneurial leadership, while differentiated, is fundamentally different than men's. It is apparent that some entrepreneurial women are crafting new visions and models of leadership, and many are experiencing unique processes entwining the developing self, values of work, life, and family, and the personal dynamics of change with the processes of developing and leading a business. These phenomena deserve careful and critical exploration if we are to understand radical changes now occurring in women business owners' work-lives and leadership development, and develop new conceptual frames and vocabulary for naming these changes as they emerge.

5

Women's Entrepreneurship Development (WED)

The ILO's Women's Entrepreneurship Development programme (ILO-WED) is part of the Small Enterprise Development Programme (SEED). ILO-WED works on enhancing economic opportunities for women by carrying out affirmative action's in support of women starting, formalizing and growing their enterprises, and by mainstreaming gender equality issues into the ILO's work in enterprise development. This approach to WED is highlighted in the ILO WED Strategy that was adopted by the Governing Body in March, 2008.

The ILO-WED approach is threefold, working with governments, employers' organizations, trade unions, and local community-based organizations to: create an enabling environment for WED that generates quality jobs; build institutional capacity in WED; and development of tools and support services for women entrepreneurs. It does so both through targeted approaches and gender mainstreaming, with a clear objective to contribute towards gender equality and women's economic empowerment.

ILO WED Strategy was built from the expertise developed under WEDGE,. WEDGE is comprised of technical cooperation projects that are funded by donors such as Irish Aid and NORAD and enable the WED strategy to be operationalized. Building on local partnerships, WEDGE projects have developed a series of tools and approaches, based on the research and experience from pilot projects organized with local partners and country offices.

WED has been working with the ILO's SKILLS department to mainstream disability into women's entrepreneurship development, targeting women with disabilities and HIV/AIDS within WEDGE projects. The WED Strategy provides a flexible and innovative response to promote women's entrepreneurship development based on local needs and circumstances. Gender Equality is and will remain at the forefront of the WED strategy.

Where we work

ILO-WED works in partnership with constituents, relevant institutions, community organizations and other UN agencies, Currently, the ILO has projects across Africa, Asia and the Middle East. Special attention has been given to Developing Entrepreneurship among Women with Disabilities and mainstreaming disability into the ILO-WED work.

What's new?

Event

Global Entrepreneurship Week 2012: Town Hall Meeting on Women's Empowerment through Entrepreneurship

Organized to mark Global Entrepreneurship Week (12-18 November 2012), the UN community alongside the missions of Ireland, Mexico and the United States to the UN, decided to hold a special event in Geneva devoted to women's entrepreneurship.

Document

Decent Work and Women's Economic Empowerment: Good Policy and Practice

A UN Women - ILO Policy Brief

The Women's Entrepreneurship Development programme referred to in the brief as a measure to be undertaken to help generating jobs and ensuring decent work for women, particularly in the informal sector.

News item

Promoting Gender Equality:

ILO Training on Gender Sensitive Value Chain Analysis in Pakistan

A 5-day training organized by the ILO "Promoting Gender Equality for Decent Employment" project and funded by the Canadian International Development Agency: CIDA.

News item

Action My Business Growth:

ILO Training for Women Entrepreneurs in Malawi

A training organized through the ILO WEDGE-SA project supporting women's entrepreneurship development in Southern Africa and funded by the Norwegian Agency for Development Cooperation: Norad.

Women" as Entrepreneurs in India:

Women owned businesses are highly increasing in the economies of almost all countries. The hidden entrepreneurial potentials of women have gradually been changing with the growing sensitivity to the role and economic status in the society. Skill, knowledge and adaptability in business are the main reasons for women to emerge into business ventures. 'Women Entrepreneur' is a person who accepts challenging role to meet her personal needs and become economically independent. A strong desire to do something positive is an inbuilt quality of entrepreneurial women, who is capable of contributing values in both family and social life. With the advent of media, women are aware of their own traits, rights and also the work situations. The glass ceilings are shattered and women are found indulged in every line of business from pappad to power cables. The challenges and opportunities provided to the women of digital era are growing rapidly that the job seekers are turning into job creators. They are flourishing as designers, interior decorators, exporters, publishers, garment manufacturers and still exploring new avenues of economic participation. In India, although women constitute the majority of the total population, the entrepreneurial world is still a male dominated one. Women in advanced nations are recognized and are more prominent in the business world. But the Indian women entrepreneurs are facing some major constraints like –

RELATED ARTICLES

Elimination of Unemployment through creating Entrepreneurs

Entrepreneurship in India

Role of Entrepreneur and Entrepreneurship

a) **Lack of confidence** – In general, women lack confidence in their strength and competence. The family members and the society are reluctant to stand beside their entrepreneurial growth. To a certain extent, this situation is changing among Indian women and yet to face a tremendous change to increase the rate of growth in entrepreneurship.

b) **Socio-cultural barriers** – Women's family and personal obligations are sometimes a great barrier for succeeding in business career. Only few women are able to manage both home and business efficiently, devoting enough time to perform all their responsibilities in priority.

c) **Market-oriented risks** – Stiff competition in the market and lack of mobility of women make the dependence of women entrepreneurs on middleman indispensable. Many business women find it difficult to capture the market and make their products popular. They are not fully aware of the changing market conditions and hence can effectively utilize the services of media and internet.

d) **Motivational factors** – Self motivation can be realized through a mind set for a successful business, attitude to take up risk and behavior towards the business society by shouldering the social responsibilities. Other factors are family support, Government policies, financial assistance from public and private institutions and also the environment suitable for women to establish business units.

e) **Knowledge in Business Administration** – Women must be educated and trained constantly to acquire the skills and knowledge in all the functional areas of business management. This can facilitate women to excel in decision making process and develop a good business network.

f) **Awareness about the financial assistance** – Various institutions in the financial sector extend their maximum support in the form of incentives, loans, schemes etc. Even then every woman entrepreneur may not be aware of all the assistance provided by the institutions. So the sincere efforts taken towards women entrepreneurs may not reach the entrepreneurs in rural and backward areas.

g) **Exposed to the training programs** - Training programs and workshops for every type of entrepreneur is available through the social and welfare associations, based on duration, skill and the purpose of the training program. Such programs are really useful to new, rural and young entrepreneurs who want to set up a small and medium scale unit on their own.

h) **Identifying the available resources** – Women are hesitant to find out the access to cater their needs in the financial and marketing areas. In spite of the mushrooming growth of associations, institutions, and the schemes from the government side, women are not enterprising and dynamic to optimize the resources in the form of reserves, assets mankind or business volunteers.

Highly educated, technically sound and professionally qualified women should be encouraged for managing their own business, rather than dependent on wage employment outlets. The unexplored talents of young women can be identified, trained and used for various types of industries to increase the productivity in the industrial sector. A desirable environment is necessary for every woman to inculcate entrepreneurial values and involve greatly in business dealings. The additional business opportunities that are recently approaching for women entrepreneurs are:

- Eco-friendly technology
- Bio-technology
- IT enabled enterprises
- Event Management
- Tourism industry
- Telecommunication
- Plastic materials
- Vermiculture
- Mineral water
- Sericulture
- Floriculture
- Herbal & health care
- Food, fruits & vegetable processing

Empowering women entrepreneurs is essential for achieving the goals of sustainable development and the bottlenecks hindering their growth must be eradicated to entitle full participation in the business. Apart from training programs, Newsletters, mentoring, trade fairs and exhibitions also can be a source for entrepreneurial development. As a result, the desired outcomes of the business are quickly achieved and more of remunerative business opportunities are found. Henceforth, promoting entrepreneurship among women is certainly a short-cut to rapid economic growth and development. Let us try to eliminate all forms of gender discrimination and thus allow 'women' to be an entrepreneur at par with men.

Women entrepreneurship

In the present globalised scenario ,women entrepreneurs are playing important role in sustaining economic development and social progress .though women entrepreneurs potential has not been tapped due their lower social status .The government through its Five Year Plans has ensured development of women entrepreneurship in India. With liberalization of economy in 1991 women entrepreneurs in Ranchi and in Jharkhand had various opportunities in the field of beauty and health care ,professions like chartered accountants ,education with opening of play schools and running lodges and girls hostels, boutiques, travel agencies and cafes in different localities of Ranchi. Some of prominent women entrepreneurs are Arti verma, Ranchi's women architect .She started her firm in 2001 with two clients and she has own firm associated with big projects. Anjali Jain is a renowned chartered accountant, who initially did not get client because she was women professional .But now she runs her own firm which has turnover of 15 to 20 lakhs per year. Sangeeta Raj and Geeta Das are successfully running schools in Ranchi.

Nisha Tulsiyan has earned the distinction of being the only women entrepreneur of Dhanbad, successfully running a bakery business .She also teaches girls and women the art of cooking so that they get employment and are able to earn their living.

Women entrepreneurs are in unorganized sector in rural area. They run small tea shops, fruit and vegetable vendors in Haat Bazaars of Mandar, Brambe, Kanke, and Murgu. These are villages of Ranchi district.

Factors influencing Women Entrepreneurs

The following are major factors influencing women entrepreneurs: -

- Economic independence
- Self-identity

- Self-confidence
- Self-motivation
- Achievement of Excellence
- Developing risk taking ability
- Equal status in society
- Greater freedom and mobility
- Prospects for Women Entrepreneurs

Women are economic force to reckon with in rural as well as in urban areas contributing in their own way to the economic growth of the country and raising their social status in their house hold, villages, cities, towns and communities.

In the present global economy the women entrepreneurs have several opportunities. They require help from Government and Self Help Groups in terms of financing and training in business so that their creative ideas are realized and emotional support and confidence from the family and society.

But they are certain drawbacks which have to be taken care off. They lack credit facilities from banks, basic education in business and marketing opportunities for their products.

To conclude in other words we can say emancipation or empowerment of women is essential prerequite for economic development and social progress of the nation in this era of globalization.

Significance of study

To paraphrase Gertrude Stein, "An entrepreneur is an entrepreneur is an entrepreneur," and it should not matter what size, shape, color, or sex the entrepreneur might be. If so, good research on entrepreneurs should generate theory applicable to all. While research shows similarities in the personal demographics of men and women entrepreneurs, there are differences in business and industry choices, financing strategies, growth patterns, and governance structures of female-led ventures.

Methodology

It has been taken in shape of Interviews from rural and urban women entrepreneurs of Ranchi district.

Women Entrepreneurship Development in India

Schemes for the development and promotion of women entrepreneurs: -

According to the Third All India Census of Small Scale Industries conducted in 2001-02 and subsequent estimates made, only 10.11% of the Micro and Small Enterprises in India are owned by women while 9.46% of the MSE enterprises are managed by women. As per the latest available estimates, the number of women owned and women managed enterprises is 12.99 Lakh and 12.15 Lakh respectively.

In order to encourage more and more women enterprises in the MSE sector, several schemes have been formulated by this Ministry and some more are in the process of being finalized, targeted only at the development of women enterprises in India.

It appears that we have not been able to get across these schemes to the intended audience.

The important schemes that are made specifically at women or give special benefits to women

1. **Trade related entrepreneurship assistance and development scheme for women (TREAD)**

With a view to encourage women in setting up their own ventures, government launched a Scheme, namely, "Trade Related Entrepreneurship Assistance and Development (TREAD) during the 11th Plan. The scheme envisaged economic empowerment of women through the development of their entrepreneurial skills in non-farm activities. There are three major components of the scheme;

(i) GoI grant upto 30% of the total project cost to the Nongovernment Organisations (NGOs) for promoting entrepreneurship among women. The remaining 70% of the project cost is financed by the lending agency as loan for undertaking activities as envisaged in the project.

(ii) GoI grants upto Rs.1 Lakh per programme to training institutions / NGOs for imparting training to the women entrepreneurs.

(iii) Need-based GoI grants upto Rs.5 Lakh to National Entrepreneurship Development Institutions and any other institutions of repute for undertaking field surveys, research studies, evaluation studies, designing of training modules etc.

Operationalizations of the Scheme

The scheme envisages that Women Associations/NGOs/SHGs should prepare composite bankable proposals for a group of women entrepreneurs, and submitted to the bank, which are signatories to participate in the scheme, namely, Syndicate Bank, State Bank of India, Canara Bank and Allahabad Bank. A copy of the proposal submitted to the bank should be endorsed to DC (MSME). Bank examines the proposal and issues approval. On the basis of the approval proposal considered by M/o MSME and 30% of the loan amount is sanctioned as grant and made available to the bank.

2. **Micro & Small Enterprises Cluster Development Programme (MSE-CDP) a) Existing Clusters:** A cluster is defined as a group of enterprises, normally 20 or more producing same/similar products/services. The Cluster Development Programme (CDP) being implemented envisages diagnostic study of identified clusters of traditional skill-based MSEs to identify appropriate technologies and their providers and to facilitate adoption of available technology meeting the specific needs of the end users. The Cluster Development aims at enhanced competitiveness, technology improvement,

and adoption of best manufacturing practices, marketing of products, employment generation etc. The scheme provides assistance for capacity building, common facilities, marketing, the delivery, assimilation and diffusion of the identified technology from its producers to the recipient user/cluster of small enterprises: -

Type of interventions

A) Soft Interventions:– capacity building activities in the cluster where no fixed assets is acquired or formed. Soft interventions, inter alia, include

- Diagnostic study
- Forming association-Trust building & Developing Identity
- Capacity building,
- Organizing workshops, seminars,
- Training & Exposure visits,
- Market development,
- Launch of Website,
- Common procurement,
- Common/complementary sales and branding;

In the past depending upon the type of cluster, assistance available for soft interventions has varied in the range of Rs.25 – 35 Lakh per cluster.

Currently we have an internal ceiling of Rs.10 Lakh for soft intervention under this Scheme, which we are trying to bring upwards. Clusters of women's enterprises are entitled up to 90% assistance for soft interventions.

B) Hard Interventions – These are tangible "assets" like

- Setting up of Common Facility Centre (CFCs),
- Mini Tool Rooms,
- Design Centres,

- Testing Facilities,
- Training Centre,
- R&D Centres,
- Common Raw Material Bank/Sales depot, etc.

There can be other tangible assets that could be set up by the women's Clusters, as long as they are put to common use. For hard interventions, it is necessary to form a Special Purpose Vehicle (SPV) which could be a registered society, or a cooperative society, or company, or a trust or any other legal entity — in which at least 20 to 30 members of the Cluster contribute and participate. Other Cluster members who do not join this SPV could also sign up as Users.

The Common Facility Centre that is set up by the SPV as a hard intervention is entitled to the highest level of assistance from the MSME Ministry i.e. upto 90% of the Project Cost. This covers the cost of machinery, plant, equipment, laboratory and other tangible assets. The balance 10% of the project cost would have to be contributed by the SPV or by the State government or the Local government. But land and building are not covered under this "Project Cost" and will have to be provided by the SPVs of the

C) Women's Enterprises Clusters or by the State government or by some other agency

Infrastructure Assistance Infrastructure assistance includes the construction of basic amenities like power, approach roads, drainage, water supply and storage and the like. MSME Ministry's assistance for this component is presently limited to 40% of the total cost — though we are trying to increase this level.

Only one element of Infrastructure Assistance i.e. Display or Exhibition Centres (which could consist of show-rooms with attached stores) are entitled to a higher level of assistance in so far as Women's Clusters are concerned, i.e. 90%. This Display/ Exhibition Centre could be built by the

Women's Clusters, SPV within the Cluster, or near the Cluster or even in adjoining Markets of Towns — as long as they exhibit and market the products manufactured by the Women's Clusters.

Creation of physical infrastructure:

This Ministry implemented the IID Scheme to provide developed sites with infrastructural facilities like power distribution network, water, telecommunications, drainage and pollution control facilities, roads, exhibition/display centres, raw materials, storage and marketing outlets, common service facilities and technological back-up services, etc. This scheme has been subsumed in the MSME-Cluster Development Programme.

All the features of IID Scheme have been retained.

To create physical infrastructure exclusively for women enterprises central grant of 40% of the project cost subject to a maximum of Rs.2 crore is available. The Ministry of MSME is making efforts to enhance the quantum of grant to 80% in a project of Rs.10 crore.

Operationalizations of the Scheme:-

i) A Cluster Development Executive (CDL) is required for executing and monitoring all soft interventions in a cluster. Normally, a CDE can be a DIC Officer/MSME-DI officer/retired expert or even hired person from Nongovernment Sector.

ii) The hard interventions in a cluster and creation of physical infrastructure require setting up a user's body/special purpose vehicle which could be society/trust/company to be formed by the cluster beneficiaries.

3. **Credit Guarantee Fund Scheme:-** The Government introduced the Credit Guarantee Fund Scheme for Small Industries in May, 2000 with the objective of making

available credit to SSI units, particularly tiny units, for loans up to Rs. 25 Lakh without collateral/ third party guarantees. The Scheme is being operated by the Credit Guarantee Fund Trust for Small Industries (CGTSI) set up jointly by the Government of India and SIDBI. The Scheme provides for collateral free credit facility (term loan and / or working capital) extended by eligible lending institutions to new and existing SSI units/ Small Scale Service and Business (industry related) Enterprises (SSSBEs) including Information Technology and Software Industry up to Rs. 25 Lakh per borrowing unit. In the case of women enterprises, the guarantee cover is up to 80% of the credit subject to maximum guarantee limit 4 of Rs. 20 Lakh. The member lending institutions (MLI) availing of guarantee from the Trust has to pay a one-time guarantee fee of 1.5% of the credit facility sanctioned by the lending institution to the borrower and annual service fee of 0.75% per annum on the amount of credit facility extended by the MLI, which is covered under the scheme.

Operationalizations of the Scheme: -

The entrepreneurs whose bank finance is approved by the lending bank may ask the bank to obtain guarantee from the Credit Guarantee Trust Fund. This facility is available online to the lending banks and clearance from the Trust is conveyed in a day or two.

4. **Support for Entrepreneurial and Managerial Development MSME Dis** regularly conduct EDPs/MDPs for existing and prospective entrepreneurs and charge fee for such courses. To encourage more entrepreneurs from among the SC/ST, women and physically challenged groups, it is proposed that such beneficiaries will not be charged any fees but, instead paid a stipend of Rs.500/- per capita per month. 50,000 entrepreneurs will be trained in IT, Fashion Technology, Catering, Agro & Food Processing, Pharmaceutical; biotechnology etc. through specialized courses run by MSME DIs. 20% of courses conducted by

these Institutions shall be exclusively for women.

5. **Exhibitions for Women under Promotional Package for MICRO & Small Enterprises Approved by CCEA under Marketing Support DC (MSME)** has formulated a scheme for women entrepreneurs to encourage Small & Micro manufacturing units owned by women in their efforts at tapping and developing overseas markets, to increase participation of representatives of small/micro manufacturing enterprises under SIDO stall at International Trade Fairs/Exhibitions, to enhance export from such units.

Under this scheme participation of women entrepreneurs in 25 international exhibitions is envisaged during the 11th Plan.

For the year 2007-08 a good number of prominent women entrepreneur associations have been requested to sponsor their members for participation in 5 international exhibitions scheduled during the months of Jan.-March, 2008. An advertisement has also been released in this regard in daily newspaper.

You will be happy to know that with a view to encourage women entrepreneurs to participate in the International Exhibitions it has been decided to:

i) Provide rent free space in the exhibitions 5
ii) Reimburse 100% economy class air fare for one representative
iii) Reimburse shipping cost upto Rs.15, 000/-

The overall ceiling shall however be Rs. 1.25 lac.

We find that in spite of the provisions available in the above mentioned schemes, the existing as well as the prospective women entrepreneurs have not derived much benefit. I would, therefore, request you to inform your members, prepare and submit suitable proposals to take as much benefit as possible. In case you require any further information or details of these schemes, you are welcome to get in touch with the MSME-DI in your state, check our website: www.smallindustryindia.com or send an email to me

6
ENTREPRENEURSHIP IN ASIAN DEVELOPING COUNTRIES

Introduction

In Asian developing countries, entrepreneurship development is currently an important issue related to economic development in the countries. It is publicly believed that the lack of entrepreneurship together with limited capital, skilled workers and technology have been the main important causes of relatively economic backwardness in most of these countries. Realizing this, training in entrepreneurship has been included as an important part of government programs to support the development of small and medium enterprises (SMEs) in the Asian developing countries. Women entrepreneurship development in Asian developing countries is currently very important since it is part of ongoing national efforts to alleviate poverty in developing countries in relation to the Millennium Development Goals (MDGs). Greater opportunities for women to participate in economic activities either as well-paid employees or as successful entrepreneurs certainly will help much in poverty reduction. Since entrepreneurship development is usually associated with SME development, this paper focuses on women entrepreneurs in SMEs.

Methodology

This paper is based on a review of key literature and a descriptive analysis of secondary data, from government sources as well as from International Labour Organization (ILO), or from individual case studies, on women entrepreneurs in Asian developing countries. Since not all countries in the region have enough data and literature, this study only covers all member countries of the Association of Southeast Asian Nations (ASEAN), China and some countries in the South Asia including India and Pakistan

Definitions and main characteristics of SMES

The definition and concept of SMEs vary between countries in the region. There is no common agreement on what distinguishes a microenterprise (MIE) from a small enterprise (SE), or a SE from a medium enterprise (ME), and a ME from a large enterprise (LE). In general, however, a MIE employs less than five (5) full time equivalent employees, although many enterprises of this category do not hire workers, often called self-employment enterprises; sometimes they use family members as helpers or unpaid workers. A SME can range from less than 100 workers in, for instance, Indonesia, to as much as 3000 laborers in China. In Indonesia, Les are those with 100 workers or more, while in Vietnam, they are units with 300 or more full time employees. Comparison between countries becomes more difficult since in some countries, definition of SME based on number of employees, value of fixed or productive assets (excluding land and building) varies, or annual revenues also vary between sectors, e.g. Thailand, India and China, or even among departments or agencies, e.g. Indonesia and Pakistan.

Definitions of SME in some Asian developing countries

While it should be intuitively evident that SMEs are of special importance to private sector growth, there is considerable disagreement within development policy circles as to why, or even whether, this is so. What are the claims that SMEs are more efficient at creating quality jobs, are more innovative, or grow faster than larger firms have been questioned on the basis of large regression analyses or on the basis of examining company registrations and corporate failures? Arguments that the overall business environment in any given country is of greater importance than the development of the SME sector have apparently caused some in development to question whether taxpayer or foundation moneys should be spent on SME initiatives. The result is that the relative priority of SMEs, and therefore SME-related policy, in development is currently unclear.

A major contributing factor towards this lack of clarity is that few of these studies have used an informed definition of the "SMEs". Within the current debate over SMEs we suggest that there are four questions of fundamental significance that should encourage the development community to discuss and determine what the definition of SMEs should be. Once there is a clearer focus on the definition, then the appropriate policy towards SMEs in developing markets will also become clearer. The four key questions are:

1. Where do large firms come from?
2. How does a country best diversify its economy?
3. Which group of businesses, by size and degree of development, has the greatest incentive to insist on policy reforms and accountable, transparent government?
4. What, in its essence, is an SME?

Besides using number of employees, annual revenues, or value of invested capital as criterion to define MIEs, SEs and MEs, in fact, MIEs can be obviously distinguished from SEs or MEs by looking at their different characteristics in many business aspects, such as market orientation, social-economic profiles of owners, nature of employment, organization and management system, degree of mechanization (nature of production process), sources of raw materials and capital, location, external relationships, and degree of involvement of women as entrepreneurs.

Main characteristics of MIEs, SEs, and MEs in Asian developing countries

Aspect

MIEs SEs MEs

1. Formality
   - Operate in informal sector, unregistered & seldom pays taxes
   - Some operate in formal
   - Sector, some unregistered & some pay taxes
   - All operate in formal sector, all registered & all pay taxes
2. Organization and management
   - Run by the owner, no division of internal labor, no formal management & no formal accounting system
   - Run by the owner, no division of labor, no formal management, and no formal accounting system
   - Many hire professional managers, have division of labor, formal organizational structure & formal account-ting system
3. Nature of employment
   - Majority use unpaid family members
   - Some hire wage laborers
   - All hire wage laborers & some have formal recruitment system
4. Nature of production process
   - Degree of mechanization very low/mostly manual & level of technology very low
   - Some use up-to-date machines
   - Many have high degree of mechanization/have access to modern technology
5. Market orientation
   - Majority sell to local market and for low-income consumers
   - Many sell to domestic market and export & many serve also middle to high-income group

- All sell to domestic market and many also export, all serve middle and high income consumers

6. Social and economic profiles of owners
   - Low or uneducated, from poor households & main motivation: survival
   - Some have good education and from non-poor households & many have business/profit motivation
   - Majority have good education
   - Many are from wealthy families & main motivation: profit
7. Sources of raw materials and capital
   - Majority use local raw materials and use own money
   - Some import raw materials & some have access to formal credits
   - Many use imported raw Materials & majority have access to formal credits
8. External relationships
   - Majority have no access to government programs and not business linkages with LEs
   - Many have good relations with government and have business linkages with LEs.
   - Majority has good access to government programs & many have business linkages with LEs.
9. Women entrepreneurs
   - Ratio of female to male as entrepreneurs is high
   - Ratio of female to male as entrepreneurs is high
   - Ratio of female to male as entrepreneurs is low

Recent development of SMEs

Asian developing countries have touted SMEs as the engine of economic growth and development, the backbone of national economies, the highest employment-generators, and a potential tool of poverty alleviation by creating self-employment avenues

In Southeast Asian countries alone (that is Indonesia, Malaysia, Thailand, Singapore, the Philippines, Brunei Darussalam, Lao PDR, Cambodia, Vietnam, and Myanmar), notwithstanding various definitional issues and data problems, by combining all sources which are available; there is an estimated total of around 52 million SMEs, with Indonesia as the largest contributor According to a report from the Secretary of the Association of Southeast Asian Nations (ASEAN) (ASEAN Development Blueprint for SMEs 2004-2014), these enterprises employ about 75-90% of the domestic workforce, especially adult persons and women. These enterprises play strategic roles in private sector development, especially in the aftermath of the 1997 Asian Financial Crisis. In some member countries, as their economies modernize or industrialize, SME provide the much-needed inter-firm linkages required to support LEs to ensure that they remain competitive in the world markets.

Number of SMEs in selected Asian developing countries: -

Name of the Country	Number ('000)	% of total enterprises
Indonesia	48,936.80	99.9
Malaysia	519.00	99.2
Philippines	72.70	99.5
Thailand	2,274.53	99.8
Vietnam	98.23	96.8
Cambodia	28.75	99
Lao PDR	26	99.4
China	2,370.26	99.7
India	12.34	90.0 -99.7
Pakistan	2,880.00	90.0
Bangladesh	5,000.00	99.0
Singapore	72.00	97.8
Nepal	3,485	98

SMEs' contribution to total value added or gross domestic product (GDP), on the other hand, are much smaller than their share in total employment. This is indeed a general characteristic of SMEs in developing countries as compared to those in developed countries. In developing countries, SMEs are not yet so important from output contribution perspective due to their low productivity because they lack advanced technologies, sophisticated methods of production and skilled workers. However, in some individual countries, SMEs have GDP shares on average above 50%, such as Cambodia at almost 77% in 2001, Indonesia which reached almost 57% in 2003, and Brunei at 66% in 1995. In China, the ratio is about 60%.

Development of women entrepreneurship

As in other parts of the world, women's entrepreneurship development in Asian developing countries has also a tremendous potential in empowering women and transforming society in the region. Yet in many countries, especially where the level of economic development, reflected by the level of income per capita and the degree of industrialization, is still low, this potential remains largely untapped. Sinhal observed that there are less than 10% of the entrepreneurs in South Asia. They comprise Bangladesh, Bhutan, India, Maldives, Nepal, Pakistan and Sri Lanka.

Categories of Women Entrepreneurs

There are three categories of women entrepreneurs, that is. "Chance", "forced" and "created" entrepreneurs.

Categories of women entrepreneurs in Asian developing countries

Category Main reason/motivation

Chance entrepreneurs

- to keep busy
- was hobby/special interest

- family/spouse had business

Forced entrepreneurs

- financial/needed the money
- control over time/flexibility
- challenge, try something on one's own
- show others I could do it

Created or pulled entrepreneurs

- to be independent & self satisfaction
- example to children
- employment to others /do something worthwhile

These different categories are based on how their businesses got started, or the main reasons or motivations behind starting their own businesses. Chance entrepreneurs are those who start a business without any clear goals or plans. Their businesses probably evolved from hobbies to economic enterprises over time. Forced entrepreneurs are those who were compelled by circumstances to start a business, their primary motivation, hence, tend to be financial. Created entrepreneurs are those who are "located, motivated, encouraged and developed" through, for instance, entrepreneurship development programs. Although, within the developing countries, the degree varies by country, depending on many factors, including level of economic development, reflected by the level of income per capita, and social, cultural and political factors. Gender equity has many dimensions and it is not easy to measure, due to the lack of accurate, gender discriminated social indicators in many countries, especially in the developing world.

Two indices often used to measure gender equity are Gender Development Index (GDI) and Gender Empowerment Measure (GEM) constructed by UNDP. GDI is human development index (HDI) adjusted for gender inequality, and HDI measures the average achievements of the country in terms of the extent to which people lead a long and healthy life, are educated and knowledgeable, and enjoy a decent standard of living. GDI measures achievements in the same basic dimensions as HDI but in addition captures inequalities between women and men. Together GDI and GEM attempt to capture the level of development of women and the extent to which women are free from discrimination in building their capabilities and in gaining access to resources and opportunities.

In 2008, the GEI ranks the 2008 situation of 157 countries, based on the most recent statistics available, and is able to determine evolution trends in 133 by comparing their present index with that of five years ago. The following table presents the GEI for selected Asian developing countries.

Gender Equity Index 2008 for selected Asian developing countries: -

Country/ Economy GEI 2008	Dimensions Education	Economic activity	Empowerment
Philippines 76	100.0	63.5	65.5
Hong Kong 72	98.5	66.5	51.8
Viet Nam 71	88.6	81.2	44.0
Thailand 70	98.7	71.7	39.7
China 69	95.1	73.3	38.2
Singapore 66	89.6	58.6	48.7
Brunei Darussalam 63	98.7	48.4	41.2
Cambodia 60	76.3	83.5	21.0
Malaysia 58	98.1	46.6	29.1
Korea, Rep. 54	84.2	53.9	23.5
Sri Lanka 53	83.7	42.9	32.1
Indonesia 52	91.7	52.8	12.4
Bangladesh 51	82.3	53.5	17.6
Nepal 44	61.1	57.0	15.3
Pakistan 42	73.2	34.2	17.5
India 40	77.5	36.6	6.3

World Economic Forum (WEF) also produces annual report on global gender gap ranking, based on gender gap index (GGI). The index is based on four critical areas of inequality between men and women:

- Economic participation and opportunity: outcomes on salaries, participation levels and access to high-skilled employment.
- Educational attainment: outcomes on access to basic and higher level education.
- Political empowerment: outcomes on representation in decision-making structures.
- Health and survival: outcomes on life expectancy and sex ratio.

The index scores are on a 0 to 1 scale (0.00 = inequality, 1.00 = equality) but can be roughly interpreted as the percentage of the gender gap that has been closed. The index scores can be interpreted as the percentage of the gap between women and men that has been closed.

Another important institution which produces annual report on global employment trends for women is the International Labour Office (ILO). Its 2008 report shows that most regions in the world are making progress in increasing the number of women in decent employment, but that full gender equality in terms of labour market access and conditions of employment has not yet been attained. According to the report, economic empowerment for women has a lot to do with their ability or inability to participate in labour markets and with the conditions of employment that the women who do manage to find work face. The report shows that labour force participation rates in South Asia have traditionally been low due to the low rates for women. Compared to 100 men active on labour markets only 42 women participate by either working or looking for work. The low participation is also reflected in the employment-to-population ratios: in 2007, only 3.4 out of 10 women of working-age actually worked (34.1%), and over the last ten years the female employment-to-population ratio slightly decreased. For the same period, the share of women as own-account workers, increased by 7.9% and as employer declined by 0.2% m.

Distribution of female status in employment in South Asia, 2007 (% change from 1997 in parentheses)

Whereas, according to the report, East Asia, which has been the most successful region in terms of economic growth over the last decade, is also the region with the highest regional labour force participation rate for women, low unemployment rates for both women and men and relatively small gender gaps in sectoral as well as status distribution. In this region, the gender gap in economically active females per 100 males continues to be among the smallest in the world. For every 100 active men, there are 79 women participating in labour markets. Between 1997 and 2007, the shares of women as own-account workers and as employer, respectively, increased by 11.1% and declined by 0.9%.

Distribution of female status in employment in East Asia, 2007 (% change from 1997 in parentheses)

Those changes in shares of women as own-account workers and employers can be seen as the development of women entrepreneurship.

Unfortunately, only few countries have national data and enough literature on women entrepreneurs, including Indonesia and Pakistan. In Indonesia, women entrepreneurs especially in SMEs have also been increasing since the 1980s during the new order era when the country achieved rapid economic growth leading to rapid increase in per capita income. Data from the National state of the art of women entrepreneurship participation, then the table may suggest that becoming an entrepreneur, especially in larger, modern and more complex Labour Survey confirm this, looking at self-employed category by gender. Although, there are more males than females who are self-employed in businesses with or without employees, or the share of females engaged in businesses is lower than that of male entrepreneurs. According to a number of studies, the reason for the increasing number of women owned enterprises are partly due to the increase of women's educational level, and to the economic pressure the women faced in their households.

With respect to sectoral distribution within the manufacturing industry, most of the women entrepreneurs are in the food, beverages and tobacco industry, followed by textile, garment and leather, and non-metallic mineral products. In basic metal and fabricated metal products, the proportion of women entrepreneurs is always very small, not more than 1%. This indicates that women entrepreneurs in manufacturing industry tend to do businesses that do not require high skills and expertise. Indeed, in Indonesia, beyond the manufacturing industry, women entrepreneurs are more likely than male to be involved in these sectors, mostly as own account traders having small shops or as owners of small restaurants or hotel.

In Pakistan, the rate of women as employers in the past 10 years does not change; while, that of those as self employed increased slightly. One important indication from this survey is that women working as entrepreneurs are still lower than that of their male counterparts. As in other countries in the region, women entrepreneurs in Pakistan are mainly found in MIEs.

Main barriers faced by women entrepreneurs in the study area

In Asian developing countries, as in any other part of the world, though the entrepreneurial process is the same for men and women, there are however, in practice, many problems faced by women, which are of different dimensions and magnitudes, which prevent them from realizing their full potential as entrepreneurs. Entrepreneurship by definition implies being in control of one's life and activeties. It is precisely this independence that societies in the region have denied women. According to Sinhal, the situation is more critical in South Asian countries, as compared to other parts of Asia. The business environment for women, which reflects the complex interplay of different factors in the South Asian region ultimately results in the disadvantaged status of women in society.

In Bangladesh, a large number of women's enterprises are operating on an informal basis and they are not identified in the country's economy. These enterprises lack the basic forms and information, marketing opportunities, regulatory and social supports.

In Nepal problems faced by women entrepreneurs in Nepal are mainly low access to credit and marketing networks, lack of access to land and property and reduced risk-taking capacity, lack of access to modern technology, lack of personal security and risk of sexual harassment, severe competition from organized units both in the domestic as well as the international markets, low level of self-confidence, and social and cultural barriers such as exclusive responsibility for household work, restrictions on mobility.

In Pakistan, Roomi and Parrot found that women entrepreneurs do not enjoy the same opportunities as men due to a number of deep-rooted discriminatory socio-cultural values and traditions. These restrictions can be observed within the support mechanism that exists to assist such fledgling businesswomen. The economic potential of female entrepreneurs is not being realized as they suffer from a lack of access to capital, land, business premises, information technology, training and agency assistance. Inherent attitudes of a patriarchal society, that men are superior to women and that women are best suited to be homemakers, create formidable challenges. Women also receive little encouragement from some male family members, resulting in limited spatial mobility and a dearth of social capital. Their research suggests that in order to foster development, multiagency cooperation is required. The media, educational policy makers and government agencies could combine to provide women with improved access to business development services and facilitate local, regional and national networks. This would help integration of women entrepreneurs into the mainstream economy.

In Indonesia, the low representative of women entrepreneurs can be attributed to at least four main factors.

First, low level of education and lack of training opportunities

It is especially true for women living in rural areas or in relatively backward provinces. This fact is consistent with a report on gender mainstreaming in the education system in Indonesia cited in Suharyo which shows that, the illiteracy rate for women is still higher than men, and the gap between men and women in rural areas is much higher than that in urban areas.

Secondly, heavy household chores place a demand on women especially those in rural areas who have more children. They are required to perform their traditional role as housewives and therefore, they have fewer hours of free time than men, both during the weekend and on weekdays.

Thirdly, there may be legal, traditions, customs, cultural or religious constraints on the extent to which women can open their own businesses. Especially in rural areas rather isolated from big cities like Jakarta. Islamic-based norms have stronger influence on women daily life. This makes female behavior or attitude in rural areas less open than male to "doing modern business" culture. In such society, women must fully comply with their primary duty as their husband's partner and housewife, they are not allowed to start their own businesses or to do jobs that involve contact with or managing men, or simply they are not allowed to leave the home alone.

Fourthly, there is lack of access to formal credit and financial institutions. This is indeed a key concern of women business owners, in fact not only in Indonesia but also in other Asian developing countries. This is found to be more problematic for women in rural areas or outside of major metropolitan areas such as Jakarta and Surabaya.

In Malaysia, the problems faced by women entrepreneurs are the same as those in Indonesia. In addition to these problems, Ming-Yen found that women entrepreneurs in Malaysia also faced a shortage of peer support networks compared with men even though various women entrepreneurs and industry associations have been formed which generally serve as a platform for women entrepreneurs to establish networks and exchange information and experiences as well as to conduct training programmes, seminars and workshops on motivation, leadership and entrepreneur development and to provide other means of support. According to their study, this is due to the fact that women may not join these associations as they might be overloaded with business and family responsibilities. This limits the women entrepreneurs' ability to seek informal advice and peers financing as well as the information networks needed for survival and growth. This might pose a challenge to women entrepreneurs in establishing networks which are helpful to the survival of their businesses.

Conclusion

Based on limited data and literature, this paper has tried to examine the participation of women as entrepreneurs in SMEs in Asian developing countries. The main issue of women entrepreneurship development discussed in this paper is the main constraints facing women to become entrepreneurs or existing women entrepreneurs to sustain or grow. The paper shows a number of interesting facts. In Asian developing countries, as they accounted, on average, for more than 95% of all firms, thus the biggest source of employment, providing livelihood for over 90% of the country's workforce, especially women and the young. Women entrepreneurs are mainly found in MIEs that is, traditional and low income generating activities. Majority of women entrepreneurs in the region were not drawn to entrepreneurship by "pull" factors, such as the need for a challenge, the urge to try something on their own and to be independent, to show others that they are capable of doing well in business, to be recognized by the society, hobby, or to use spare time, but by "push" factors such as poverty, unemployment, the need to have more cash income to support the family daily expenditures, and precaution motives. This may suggest that when women in the region are better educated and have greater well-paid employment opportunities, their participation in SMEs may decline.

7

WOMEN ENTREPRENEURSHIP IN INDIA: OPPORTUNITIES AND CHALLENGES

Social and economic development of women is essential for overall economic development of any society or a country. During the last two decades, increasing numbers of Indian women entered the field of entrepreneurship and also they are gradually changing the face of business both literally and figuratively. But still they have not capitalized their potential in India the way it should be.

This paper looks into opportunities and challenges that Indian women face in the entrepreneurial society; how to boost women entrepreneurial skills; what are the reasons that propel women to undertake such profession. It also seeks to find what hinders women entrepreneurship and what measures to take to remove such obstacles. In general, the paper examines various motivating and de-motivating internal and external factors affecting women entrepreneurship in India.

The paper compares early stage entrepreneurial male & female activity among Nordic countries with the same of USA. It also compares various programs& schemes developed by Nordic countries & agencies that provide support to them. The authors conclude by stating that the Nordic countries need a framework for policy learning to develop a proper a policy mix towards promoting women entrepreneurship. He suggests that this policy framework to needs to:

- Identify the reasons for women for involving themselves in entrepreneurial activities.

- Define the factors of hindrance for women entrepreneurship.
- Determine the possible success factors for women in such entrepreneurial activities.
- Make an evaluation of people's opinion about women entrepreneurship.

Woman constitutes the family, which leads to society and Nation. Social and economic development of women is necessary for overall economic development of any society or a country. Entrepreneurship is the state of mind which every woman has in her but has not been capitalized in India in way in which it should be. Due to change in environment, now people are more comfortable to accept leading role of women in our society, though there are some exceptions.

Our increasing dependency on service sector has created many entrepreneurial opportunities especially for women where they can excel their skills with maintaining balance in their life.

Propose of this empirical study is intended to find out various motivating and de-motivating internal and external factors of women entrepreneurship. It is an attempt to quantify some for non parametric factors to give the sense of ranking these factors. It will also suggest the way of eliminating and reducing hurdles of the women entrepreneurship development in Indian Context.

Introduction

Entrepreneurship refers to the act of setting up a new business or reviving an existing business so as to take advantages from new opportunities. Thus, entrepreneurs shape the economy by creating new wealth and new jobs and by inventing new products and services. However, an insight study reveals that it is not about making money, having the greatest ideas, knowing the best sales pitch, applying the best marketing strategy. It is in reality an attitude to create something new and an activity which creates value in the entire social eco-system. It is the psyche makeup of a person. It is a state of mind, which develops naturally, based on his/ her surrounding and experiences, which makes him/ her think about life and career in a given way.

The women have achieved immense development in their state of mind. With increase in dependency on service sector, many entrepreneurial opportunities especially for women have been created where they can excel their skills with maintaining balance in their life. Accordingly, during the last two decades, increasing numbers of Indian women have entered the field of entrepreneurship and also they are gradually changing the face of business of today, both literally and figuratively. But still they have not capitalized their potential in India the way it should be.

The first part of this paper deals with the ideas why to boost the women entrepreneurship and what are the reasons that propel women to undertake such profession. This part also depicts the factors of hindrance of women entrepreneurship and also the likely measures to be taken for removing such obstacles that are affecting women entrepreneurship.

The second part deals with a review of various research studies done on women entrepreneurship along with study on their impact on various economies. The third part deals with objectives and research methodologies. The fourth part concentrates on analysis of data collected through questionnaires to establish motivating and de-motivating internal and external factors of women entrepreneurship. The attempt has been made to rank these factors in regard to their severity of impact on women entrepreneurship. The last part of this study includes the suggestive measures for eliminating and reducing the hurdles for the women entrepreneurship development in Indian context.

Reasons for Boosting Women Entrepreneurship

The role of women entrepreneurs in the process of

economic development has been recognized form nineties in various parts of the world. Today, in the world of business, women entrepreneurship has become an essential movement in many countries and has been accepted in all areas of working. The United Nations report has also concluded that economic development is closely related to the advancement of women. In nations where women have advanced, economic growth has usually been steady. By contrast, in countries where women have been restricted, the economy has been stagnant. The data on correlation between Genders related development index and GDP per capital reinforces the above fact

TABLE NO. 1

Gender Related Development Index and its Component: -

Rank	Country	Gender related development index	As a per % of HDI	GDP per Capital (US$)
1	Australia	0.966	98.9	34923
2	Norway	0.961	99.6	53433
3	Iceland	0.959	99.0	44613
4	Canada	0.959	99.2	35812
5	Sweden	0.956	99.3	36712
6	France	0.956	99.4	33674
7	Netherland	0.954	98.9	38694
8	Finland	0.954	99.5	34526
9	Spain	0.949	99.4	31560
10	Ireland	0.948	98.2	44613
114	India	0.594	97.1	4102

As shown in the above table, Gender related development index is significantly correlated with GDP per capita. The value of correlation coefficient comes 0.857371. Therefore, it can be treated as one of the parameter to show the economic condition & growth of the country.

Business association and Women Entrepreneurship:

Structural association and group of people also promote women entrepreneurship. A vital link to economic decision-making processes, the business associations has made their members' visions and priorities a part of the national political and economic agenda. Around the globe many more organizations are contributing in similar ways. Table 2 depicts some of the business associations of some countries.

These associations undertake wide varieties of activities encompassing credit, business skill training, technical and technology training, employment creation, marketing services, legal assistance, psychological counseling and some social welfare trade programs. These associations have also played a positive and vital role in promoting international trade for women entrepreneurs.

TABLE NO. 2

Country Business Association

- Russia Novgorod Women's Parliament,
- Perm Business Women's Club,
- St. Petersburg Institute for International Entrepreneurship Development,
- Archangelsk Women Entrepreneurs,
- Novosibirsk Association of Women Entrepreneurs
- US Business and Professional Women,
- National Association of Women Business Owners (NAWBO)
- Nepal Women Entrepreneurs Association of Nepal (WEAN)

- Malawi National Association of Business Women (NABW)

Reasons for Women opting for Entrepreneurship

Self determination, expectation for recognition, self esteem and career goal are the key drivers for taking up entrepreneurship by women. Sometimes, women chose such career path for discovering their inner potential, caliber in order to achieve self satisfaction. It can also provide a mean to make best use of their leisure hours.

However, dismal economic conditions of the women arising out of unemployment in the family and divorce can compel women into entrepreneurial activities

Obstacles for Women Entrepreneurs

The entrepreneurial process is same for men and women. Successful men and women entrepreneurs undergo similar motivations and thus achieve success in largely same way under similar challenges. They are also found to have access to fund from the same sources. The same condition both men and women can be successful entrepreneurs. However, in practice most of the upcoming women entrepreneurs face problems that are of different dimensions and magnitudes than that faced by their male counterparts. These problems, generally, prevent these women entrepreneurs from realizing their potential as entrepreneurs.

The major hurdles that the women face during starting and running a company generally come from financing and balancing of life. The balancing of life is caused due to lack of family support for the women. The other hindering external factors include gender discrimination, inaccessibility to information, training opportunities, infrastructure etc. Some internal factors like risk aversion by women, lack of confidence, lack of vision of strategic leader etc. can also create obstacles for the women entrepreneurship development.

TABLE NO. 3

Snapshot of key Factors

S. N.	Country	Factors
1.	United States	access to capital, access to information, access to networks
2.	Korea	Financing, the effort to balance work and family
3.	Indonesia	Exporting their products overseas, increasing the volume of production,
4.	Vietnam	• the prevailing social and cultural gender-based inequalities and biases
		• accessing credit from formal institutions in view of their limited access to formal education, ownership of property, and social mobility
		• unequal access to opportunities and markets
		• include business experiences,
		• limited knowledge of marketing strategies,
		• weak business associations,
		• lack of networking facilities
		• poor access to education and training programmes
5.	Bangladesh	• Inadequate financing
		• Competition
		• Obtaining quality raw materials, and
		• balancing time between the enterprise and the family
6.	Uganda	• lack of training and advisory services
		• lack of managerial and technical skills,
		• weak infrastructure
		• difficulties in accessing loans, and
		• Complicated company registration processes.
7.	Rwanda	• restricted mobility
		• security
8.	Morocco	• lack of operational and managerial skills
		• Cultural constraints

		• Inefficient production mechanisms
		• lack of managerial skills
9.	Kenya	• lack of technical skills,
		• confidence,
		• strong individual involvement
		• the willingness to take risks
10.	Africa	• Constraints and barriers to obtaining money to start and grow their own business.
		• Women's inexperience of negotiating with the banks
		• Their lack of financial confidence.
		• Access to the essential abilities, skills and experiences for business.
		• Their dual (household) and triple (community) roles and responsibilities.
		• Lack of key dedicated "time" to be able to explore and nurture their resources.
		• Lack of abilities, skills and expertise in certain business matters.
		• lack of exposure to the world of business
11.	Mauritius	• the hassle of getting permits;
		• the lack of market;
		• the ability to raise capital;
		• Not being taken as seriously as men.

Above table depicts the various internal and external factors that affect the development of women entrepreneurship in various countries.

Literature Review

Darrene, Harpel and Mayer performed a study on finding the relationship between elements of human capital and self employment among women.

The study showed that self employed women differ on most human capital variable as compared to the salary and wage earning women. The study also revealed the fact that the education attainment level is faster for self employed women than that for other working women. The percentage of occupancy of managerial job is found to be comparatively higher in case of self employed women as compared to other working women. This study also shed light on similarity and dissimilarity of situations for self employed men and self employed women. Self employed men and women differ little in education, experience and preparedness. However, the main difference lies in occupational and industry experience. The percentage of population holding management occupation is lower for self employed women as compared to self employed men. Also the participation levels of self employed women are found to be less than of self employed men in industries like communication, transportation, wholesale trade, manufacturing and construction.

Jalbert performed a study to explore the role of women entrepreneurs in a global economy. It also examined how women's business associations can strengthen women's position in business and international trade. The analysis is performed on the basis of facts and data collected through field work (surveys, focus groups and interviews) and through examining the existing published research. The study has shown that the women business owners are making significant contributions to global economic health, national competitiveness and community commerce by bringing many assets to the global market. As per the analysis of the research study, women entrepreneurs have demonstrated the ability to build and maintain long-term relationships and networks to communicate effectively, to organize efficiently, to be fiscally conservative, and to be aware of the needs of their environment and to promote sensitivity to cultural differences.

Researchers contend that women business owners posses certain specific characteristics that promote their creativity and generate new ideas and ways of doing things. These characteristics include focus, high energy level, personal motivations, self employed father, social adroitness, interpersonal skills etc. There is a worldwide pool of economically active persons, known as the Women's Indicators and Statistical Data Base (WISTAT), from which one can extrapolate the general number of women entrepreneurs. WISTAT titles the category "employers and own-account workers," but the category could be termed as well as self employed or business owners. The category describes those who are economically independent and who could be entrepreneurs. The number of women to 100 men in each region is represented for three decades spanning 1970 to 1990. The study revealed that the gap between men and women business owners has narrowed significantly. In 1970 women numbered 26 for each 100 men, but by 1990 women numbered 40 for each 100 men who were self employed Tambunan, made a study on recent developments of women entrepreneurs in Asian developing countries. The study focused mainly on women entrepreneurs in small and medium enterprises based on data analysis and review of recent key literature. This study found that in Asian developing countries SMEs are gaining overwhelming importance; more than 95% of all firms in all sectors on average per country. The study also depicted the fact that representation of women entrepreneurs in this region is relatively low due to factors like low level of education, lack of capital and cultural or religious constraints. However, the study revealed that most of the women entrepreneurs in SMEs are from the category of forced entrepreneurs seeking for better family incomes.

Das in 2000 performed a study on women entrepreneurs of SMEs in two states of India i.e. Tamilnadu and Kerala. The initial problems faced by women entrepreneurs are quite similar to those faced by women in western countries. However, Indian women entrepreneurs faced lower level of work family conflict and are also found to differ from their counterparts in western countries on the basis of reasons for starting and succeeding in business.

Similar trends are also found in other Asian countries such as Indonesia and Singapore. Again the statistics showed that the proportion of business setup and operated by women is much lower than the figures found in western countries.

Singh identifies the reasons & influencing factors behind entry of women in entrepreneurship.

He explained the characteristics of their businesses in Indian context and also obstacles & challenges. He mentioned the obstacles in the growth of women entrepreneurship are mainly lack of interaction with successful entrepreneurs, social un-acceptance as women entrepreneurs, family responsibility, gender discrimination, missing network, low priority given by bankers to provide loan to women entrepreneurs.

He suggested the remedial measures like promoting micro enterprises, unlocking institutional frame work, projecting & pulling to grow & support the winners etc. The study advocates for ensuring synergy among women related ministry, economic ministry & social & welfare development ministry of the Government of India.

Lall & Sahai conduct a comparative assessment of multi-dimensional issues & challenges of women entrepreneurship & family business. The study identified Psychographic variables like, degree of commitment, entrepreneurial challenges & future plan for expansion, based on demographic variables.

Through stratified random sampling & convenience sampling the data have been collected from women entrepreneurs working in urban area of Lucknow.

The study identified business owner's characteristics as self perception self esteem, Entrepreneurial intensity & operational problem for future plans for growth & expansion. The study suggested that though, there has been considerable growth in number of women opting to work in family owned business but they still have lower status and face more operational challenges in running business.

Bowen & Hisrich compared & evaluated various research studies done on entrepreneurship including women entrepreneurship. It summaries various studies in this way that female entrepreneurs are relatively well educated in general but perhaps not in management skills, high in internal locus of control, more masculine, or instrumental than other women in their values likely to have had entrepreneurial fathers, relatively likely to have first born or only children, unlikely to start business in traditionally male dominated industries & experiencing a need of additional managerial training.

Women network report on Women in Business & in Decision making focus on women entrepreneurs, about their problems in starting & running the business, family back ground, education, size of business unit. Some interesting facts which came out from this report are less educated women entrepreneurs are engaged in micro enterprises, have husband & children but have no help at home. Most of the women establish enterprises before the age of 35, after gaining some experience as an employee somewhere else. The motivational factors were desire for control & freedom to take their own decision as well as earning handsome amount of money.

Dedication of more than 48 hours in a week with the family support to their enterprises gave them a sense of self confidence. However, to maintain balance between family & work life is a major challenge before women entrepreneurs especially for those who have children & working husband.

Then Cohoon, Wadhwa, and Mitchell present detailed exploration of men and women entrepreneur's motivations, background and experiences. The study is based on the data collected from successful women entrepreneurs. Out of them 59% had founded two or more companies. The study identifies top five financial & psychological factors motivating women to become entrepreneurs. These are desire to build the wealth, the wish to capitalize own business ideas they had, the appeal of startup culture, a long standing desire to own their own company and working with someone else did not appeal them. The challenges are more related with entrepreneurship rather than gender. However, the study concluded with the requirement of further investigation like why women are so much concerned about protecting intellectual capital than their counterpart. Mentoring is very important to women, which provides encouragement & financial support of business partners, experiences & well developed professional network.

Greene evaluates the research and publication contribution in the area of women entrepreneurship. The study categorized various journal & resources of research on the basis of certain parameters concerned with women entrepreneurship like gender discrimination, personal attributes, financing challenges, business unit, context and feminist perspectives.

Now, Damwad described the experiences, initiatives & obstacles faced at five Nordic countries like Finland, Denmark, Iceland, Norway & Sweden towards women entrepreneurship. It broadly identifies few obstacles like financing, lack of knowledge & skills in business life, markets & entrepreneurial activity, work life balance including lack of growth & wishes to grow and most importantly women as other groups are heterogeneous. The study compares early stage entrepreneurial male & female activity among Nordic countries with the same of USA. It also compares various programme & schemes developed by Nordic countries & agencies that provide support to them.

OECD & European Commission are focusing on methodologies in analyzing quantitative & qualitative women entrepreneurship. The Nordic countries need a framework for policy learning develop a proper policy mix towards promoting women entrepreneurship.

Objectives

- To identify the reasons for women for involving themselves in entrepreneurial activities

- To identify the factors of hindrance for women entrepreneurship
- To determine the possible success factors for women in such entrepreneurial activities.
- To make an evaluation of people's opinion about women entrepreneurship.

Methodology

The research is based on secondary & primary data. It's an exploratory & descriptive in nature. The secondary data is collected from review of past researches and other reports. The factors have been identified then classified into three categories factors responsible for hindrance, reasons for starting the business & reasons for success in women entrepreneurship. Then these factors with their sub classification rated on Likert scale of 1 to 5, where 1 denotes least important & 5 denote most important.

Then these factors have been further analyzed through Chi square test to check the difference between opinions collected from different sets of people. PSW 18 has been use for calculation purposes.

The data has been collected from the female PGDM students & faculty members only. It is just have common areas of concerns in both the sample group.

All the three forms of factors analyzed from the view points of marital status & occupation. Results show that one basis of marital status we find major differences of opinion at significance level of 5.

These are need for Money & others factors on which these two sets of people have different opinion.

However in hindrance reason we could not find any significant difference. When it comes on success factors Marketing skills & Preservation also have significant difference.

On the basis of occupation differences are more because two sets have difference in generation also.

Students & faculty members have significant differences on various issues almost in every set of factors. Starting from hindrance factors they significantly differ on Raising Capital, Information &advice, skills & expertise, Gender discriminations & others. In the second category of factors i.e. reasons for starting business factors for significant difference are passion; need for money, to become independent, self satisfaction & others. In the category of success factors difference are on the issues like quality of product & service, uniqueness of design & services, management skills & marketing skills & preservation.

Measures to Remove the Obstacles

The elimination of obstacles for women entrepreneurship requires a major change in traditional attitudes and mindsets of people in society rather than being limited to only creation of opportunities for women. Hence, it is imperative to design programmes that will address to attitudinal changes, training, supportive services. The basic requirement in development of women entrepreneurship is to make aware the women regarding her existence, her unique identity and her contribution towards the economic growth and development of country.

The basic instinct of entrepreneurship should be tried to be reaped into the minds of the women from their childhood. This could be achieved by carefully designing the curriculum that will impart the basic knowledge along with its practical implication regarding management of an enterprise.

Adopting a structured skill training package can pave the way for development of women entrepreneurship.

Such programmes can train, motivate and assist the upcoming women entrepreneurship in achieving their ultimate goals. Various schemes like the World Bank sponsored programmes can be undertaken for such purposes. The course design should focus on imparting input on profitability, marketability and practical management lessons. Besides, there should be consideration in helping the women entrepreneurs in balancing their family life and work life. As a special concern, computer illiterate women can be trained on Information Technology to take the advantage of new technology and automation.

The established and successful women entrepreneurs can act as advisors for the upcoming women entrepreneurs. The initiatives taken from these well established entrepreneurs for having interaction with such upcoming women entrepreneurs can be proved to be beneficial in terms of boosting their morale and confidence. It may result in more active involvement of women entrepreneurs in their enterprises.

Infrastructure set up plays a vital role for any enterprise. Government can set some priorities for women entrepreneurs for allocation of industrial plots, sheds and other amenities. However, precautionary measures should be undertaken to avoid the misuse of such facility by the men in the name of the women.

Even in today's era of modernization the women entrepreneurs depend on males of their family for marketing activities. This is simply because they lack the skill and confidence for undertaking such activities. Women development corporations should come forward to help the women entrepreneurs in arranging frequent exhibitions and setting up marketing outlets to provide space for the display of products or advertisement about services made by women.

Conclusion

The study tried to find out the difference among various

set of people of the crucial factors which are concerned with the women entrepreneurial opportunities at large. Issues have been identified through various review of literature. It should be cross checked with the real entrepreneurs. These factors may vary from place to place business to business but women entrepreneurship is necessary for the growth of any economy weather it large or small.

8

Effective Communication

For Women Entrepreneurs effective communication is the most important aspect in establishing an Enterprise in the private sector in India.

Last summer, I went to meet an advertising agent at his office for some business of mine. While waiting for him at the office welcome lounge, the receptionist asked me to feel free and grab a cup of coffee for myself in the meantime. Heading towards the coffee bar, here's what my eyes fell upon, a large sign board beside the snack counter which said in big bold letters, "After tea break staff should empty the teapot and stand upside down on the draining board." I gave up the coffee and darted out, making a terrible attempt to hold back my laughter. I certainly did not want to associate with such a disastrous advertising company.

Communicating effectively, whether written or spoken should be an important lesson in all personality building text books as it is an ability that's not easy to acquire but needs constant application and practice. That is why I agree with Truman Capote's thoughts about communication in his book Music for Chameleons where he says, "A conversation is a dialogue, not a monologue. That's why there are so few good conversations: due to scarcity, two intelligent talkers seldom meet."

Organizations today are also emphasizing on the aspect of effective communication when recruiting people. According to Gartner Research, global interaction skills are the top priority skills for hiring employees in the future.

Advantages of Good Communication Skills

- Good communication skills are not limited to writing, reading or talking a language. Good communication is when person A can completely transfer his/her thoughts to person B
- Good communication skills help build strong relationships thus providing you with reducing friction and confrontations
- Communication skills make you attractive and interested by the other party
- Communication is a two way process. Along with speaking your thoughts it is important to be a good listener to the other party. Thus good communication helps in clarifying ideas and thoughts
- Trust between individuals and the organization is built when they understand each other and good communication helps in doing that
- Small shortfalls and follies can be accommodated if compensated by good communication

How to make your Communication Effective

To be able to communicate an idea or conversation brilliantly, here are two important principles to follow:

1. Think before you speak – The old proverb stands true when you want to communicate well. Organize and arrange your thoughts. Break a complex thought into simpler, smaller bits before you launch into a conversation. It will allow your audience to easily absorb and grasp the details of your thoughts.
2. Listen up, don't just speak – Communication is not unidirectional. Listening attentively to what the other person has to say without interrupting is also an important attribute to communicating better. Also, don't get lost in your own internal noise or start thinking up an effective reply but focus on what the other person says.

What will eventually make a lasting impression is your command of the language you communicate in. Beef up your vocabulary so that you don't fall short of words at anytime and as Confucius rightly said, "If language is not correct, then what is said is not what is meant."

Goal Setting–The Undeveloped Project

A few years ago, my grandfather passed away. I was very close to him and the loss was irreparable for me. My days turned melancholy as I had lost my only childhood companion. Miserable and lonely the days rolled by and then one day my grandmother gave me a bunch of letters my grandfather had written to me. The letters were precious to me as his last parting gift. One of the letters was the closest to my heart as it has helped learn a very important lesson in life – the act of setting a goal and visualizing it.

Goal is the negative film of your future photograph, was one my most favourite lines in that letter. I realized that goals help you become what you want to be. They show you what mettle you're made of. When you set a goal for yourself, irrespective of whether you accomplish it or not, the act itself places the stepping stone for reaching your destination. You realize the reason for your survival through goals. However, it's always important to visualize your goal too. If you want to win that race, see yourself running that marathon and emerging a winner, leaving your opponents behind, your ears savoring the loud applause of the throng. Let the power of your imagination transport you into that dream of yours. It's absolutely magical.

Why set a goal, at all?

American Speaker and author, Jim Rohn says, "The major reason for setting a goal is for what it makes of you to accomplish it. What it makes of you will always be the far greater value than what you get." The process of goal setting and striving hard to achieve it brings out valuable qualities that are buried within every individual like determination, sincerity, leadership, discipline, the list is endless. It is also important for the following reasons:

- Goals add value to work as without a reason any activity is futile and a drag on labor
- Goals help keep our priorities and help them move to the intended path
- It helps to channelize energies and our potential
- It helps move from activity and efforts to results

How to set goals?

1. Write, draw, cut-out, photograph your goal - This is a way of sending out a message to your brain of what you want to accomplish. Keep reminding yourself of the goal. This way you won't lose focus and will gradually program yourself to move in the direction of your hunt.
2. Have a clear and to the point goal – Specifics are important when setting your goal. Timeline, numbers, weights etc. don't forget the detailing.
3. Goals should be reasonable and practical – Your goal should be believable to you without an iota of doubt whether you will be able to achieve it or not. For that reason, they should be realistic enough not to clash with your inherent values.
4. A goal without a purpose like a boat without an anchor – A purpose is the tip of the arrow of a goal; it has to be so sharp that it tears any on-road barriers to pieces. A strong purpose propels you to move forward even when the waves are against you.

That one letter has been my guiding star for years. It has helped me visualize so many snapshots of my future. It taught me that if you want to achieve something, envision your goals and you will automatically get the fuel to move on. I wish it does the same for you.

Overcoming Failures

Conquer Failure

"Never be afraid to face failure" I heard these lines oftentimes from my favorite English teacher. Its very true that when faced with a challenge to prove something, we always think and question our ability to succeed. However, this it is an act leading to failure. There is no success without failure. Great people face and overcome failure before achieving success. Understanding and accepting failure is the first step towards overcoming it. Accept failure as a temporary setback that helps move ahead with a positive attitude. Understanding failure as a stepping stone to progress is the right approach.

Learning from failures is probably the most important lesson people can use. Diving deep and understanding failure reasons and points of failure ensures that the next time around you overcome it. Most people face failures and give up and this blocks the path to success. Smart and successful people try till they win.

The first step to achieving success is to recognizing your weakness. Without understanding and accepting weaknesses it is impossible to change and move forward. Take a step back in history and you will see scores and scores of great people who realized their weakness and upon doing so translated those weaknesses to their strengths. It sounds like an exaggerated example but its true that Edison failed ten thousand times before he invented the electric bulb.

Here's how you can tackle the failure bull:

- Align your efforts and focus based on learning from mistakes and understanding weakness

- Discouragement is part of every failure and the skill to overcome it is most important to overcome failure.
- One of the most important steps to overcome failure is to start thinking positively
- Always try to stay in the company of successful and positive people. Look at positive and inspiring examples around you
- Developing persistence coupled with a positive approach to overcome failures in life.

Instill the spirit within yourself to keep trying until you succeed. Seldom you don't realize the proximity with success, so don't give yourself the chance to regret if you realized it was just around the corner when you gave up.

Overcoming Stress

The physical and mental responses to a disparity between the real and imaginary experience is called stress. When it enhances productivity it is called positive stress and in cases where stress dissipates your energy to make you less productive, it is called negative stress or depression.

Reasons for Stress

Reasons for stress vary from one to another. For someone work at office could be stressful for others it might be enjoyable. Any kind of change to which your body reacts negatively is harmful in the long run. To cope with stress, you need to discover the reasons behind it. They could be:

- Type of work
- Psychological imbalance
- Wrong food habits
- Mental Imbalance

Ways to counteract stress

Post identifying the reasons for stress you need to be vigilant and be aware of the feeling of stress. Some indicators could be; strain on different parts of the body like, eyes, neck, shoulders etc. In such circumstances, give yourself a break from the stress accelerating entity which could be an activity or a thought. Doing so will help you ease the strain away and enable you to look at the problem with a calmer and better perspective.

Here are some pointers that can help you bust the stress:

- Develop a positive approach towards life. Looking at a glass as half full than half empty is the right attitude
- Don't avoid risks. Running away from challenging situations will only worsen the condition of stress. Pluck your courage and confront it
- Move to areas of strength. Many people continue to be disturbed by stress as they work on their weaknesses and are never able to see success or reach their potential.
- Take a break when the going gets tough. Try to pamper yourself with a good massage, a peaceful nap or yoga stretches and see how rejuvenated you feel, ready to battle whatever comes your way
- Persistence is an important skill and approach in life. The ability to not give up goals and pursue even while failure stares at you is the approach which will get you out of stressful situations
- Learn to give than to take. The higher your expectations from others the more disappointed you feel when they don't stand up to those expectations
- Program your mind to look for positives in everything rather than negative.
- Read motivational books and keep company with successful people. Don't be alone while in a stressful situation. Always seek company and it will get you out of stress

Vision vs. Goals

"The vision that you glorify in your mind, the ideal that you enthrone in your heart, this you will build your life by, and this you will become." A human without a dream is almost dead. Every person needs a reason to live and they are built up of dreams. Vision in scientific terms is to see physical things. In philosophical terms it is the ability to perceive something beyond real and creates a motivation in the perceiver to live and achieve it.

Characteristics of a Vision

- A vision is the ultimate achievement which every human expects in his lifetime
- Sometimes visions are beyond a lifetime
- A vision is a construct of various thoughts and usually not very definitive and clear
- On the pyramid of life, vision is on top and out of that is derived mission and goals
- A vision may not be achieved always

Goals from Vision

Goals are the derivatives of a vision. A goal is what translates a vision to reality. When you set small objectives that are time bound and measurable and work towards reaching your vision that is what constitutes a goal. Your vision might look vague or unrealistic but your goals should be very clear and realistic to you. This will only help you to achieve what seems unachievable. A goal has the following characteristics:

- Goals are derived from vision and are achievable milestones towards the vision
- Goals are classified as short term, medium term and long term based on the strategy to achieve the vision in the most optimized way

Vision is important for not just businesses but even individuals to succeed. It is your best future state and what you actually want to be like. True leaders believe vision to be a reality that will come to existence someday. It is palpable to them and often they are so passionate about their vision that they are ready to move mountains if need be, just to transform their vision to reality.

Inculcating the Sense of Self-Employment in Indian Youth

Youth employment remains a major problem in every country including India, with its relatively larger population of people in their 20s and 30s, is no exception. Population explosion, development and increase in literacy levels ensure that a significant percentage of the youth are unemployed or underemployed. Every year, lakhs of graduates apply for and compete in national and state level examinations for jobs in the public sector, which is no longer the mass recruiter that it was a decade or two ago.

Though there has been virtually no research to measure the effect of self-employment on the long-term economy of a country, the general feeling is that it can only do good to it. Economic self-reliance can be driven only through self-employment and in diverse industries at that. The current trend in India which is mass employment in outsourced services might harm the country in the longer term with the country's economy directly affected by that of the outsourcing countries.

Education is the foremost way of inculcating entrepreneurial values in children. The stress should not only be in self-reliance but also in honesty and ethics. Vision, which is what self-employment primarily requires, is not something that can be taught but, in the current education system, all the cards are not presented on the table. The student is not made aware of possibilities.

The Indian government's programs aimed at encouraging self-employment in the youth, especially in the small industries sector, are finding major takers in the rural sector. While basic education is good to have, qualities like creativity and innovation are not necessarily driven by schooling. However, the programs tend to be too old-school and the processes bureaucratic. The designing of programs should take into account the indigenous treasures different areas hold and their success lies in harnessing that. Making these programs attractive in terms of expected returns will see more takers.

There is a way that mass-employment in outsourced services can be turned into an opportunity. There is a large pool of the urban youth that are recent graduates and are relatively inexperienced need to be trained in order to work for those MNCs. The government can tap into this pool and offer to help them setup industries related to their basic education. Instead of completely switching careers, the youth can pursue their interest right into a life-long, satisfying career.

The psychological effects of being self-reliant, becoming masters of their craft, not having to work for a large, faceless corporation, a better status in the society are some of the advantages of being self-employed. The learning involved in the setup and maintenance of industries is sure to challenge and provide enough fodder for the bright minds of our youth.

Women Entrepreneurship- Homemaker Views

Women are generally perceived as home makers with little to do with economy or commerce. But this picture is changing. In Modern India, more and more women are taking up entrepreneurial activity especially in medium and small scale enterprises.

Even as women are receiving education, they face the prospect of unemployment. In this background, self employment is regarded as a cure to generate income .The Planning commission as well as the Indian government recognizes the need for women to be part of the mainstream of economic development. Women entrepreneurship is seen as an effective strategy to solve the problems of rural and urban poverty.

Traditionally, women in India have been generally found in low productive sectors such as agriculture and household activities. Human Development Report 2004 ranks India 103 in Gender related Development Index (GDI). As per 2001 census; women constitute nearly half of India's population. Out of this total, 72% were engaged in agriculture, 21.7% in other non agricultural pursuits with only 6.3% in household industries.

Women entrepreneurs in India are handicapped in the matter of organizing and running businesses on account of their generally low levels of skills and for want of support system. The transition from homemaker to sophisticated business woman is not that easy.

But the trend is changing. Women across India are showing an interest to be economically independent. Women are coming forth to the business arena with ideas to start small and medium enterprises. They are willing to be inspired by role models- the experience of other women in the business arena.

The role of women entrepreneurs is especially relevant in the situation of large scale unemployment that the country faces. The modern large scale industry cannot absorb much of labour as it is capital intensive. The small scale industry plays an important role absorbing around 80% of the employment.

The myth that women cannot engage in productive employment needs to be dispelled. They can be encouraged to set up small and medium scale industries on their own initiative. Entrepreneurship development for women is an important factor in economic development of India.

Rural women can be encouraged to start cottage industries. Rural based micro enterprises have been encouraged by the government by various schemes-such as Integrated Rural Development Program (IRDP), Training of Rural Youth for Self Employment (TRYSEM), and Development of Women and Children in Rural Areas (DWCRA). The aim is to remove poverty through entrepreneurial programs.

An ILO report on women entrepreneurship identifies the following problems faced by women entrepreneurs.

1. Lack of family support- Sometimes the family may make the women feel guilty of neglecting household duties in her pursuit of business obligations. Cultural traditions may hold back a woman from venturing into her own business.
2. Lack of capital-traditional sources of finance like banks are reluctant to lend to women entrepreneurs especially if they do not have any male or family backing. This is especially true of lower income females. Women do not have adequate finance or legal knowledge to start an enterprise.
3. Lack of confidence and faith-lack of role models undermines the self confidence of women entrepreneurs. The activity of selling is considered abhorrent to the female gender.
4. Lack of right public/ private institutions: Most public and private incentives are misused and do not reach the woman unless she is backed by a man. Also many trade associations like ministries, chambers of commerce do not cater to women expecting women's organizations to do the necessary thing.

The government must evolve appropriate policies to help women entrepreneurs. Networking facilities must be provided as well as adequate entrepreneurship awareness training should be provided using the help of local NGOs. Credit facilities must be made available and marketing help must be provided. All these will help foster a culture of entrepreneurship among women in India.

Top Ten Women Entrepreneurs - World

Worldwide, businessmen, economists and politicians today assent that, 'Women owned businesses boost the economy'. Presenting here, dames who were/is pioneer 'women entrepreneurship' and epitomize the female power globally.

1. **Madame C.J. Walker (1867–1919)**

   Known as the first female entrepreneur, her manufacturing company developed hair care products for black women. A great philanthropist, she is opined as the first female African-American millionaire too.

2. **Gabrielle Bonheur 'Coco' Chanel (1883-1971)**

   French designer and founder of the brand 'Chanel', Coco is immortal with her perfume 'Chanel No. 5'. Her simple but elegant, stylish, sophisticated yet comfortable designs enchant the beauties even today.

3. **Estée Lauder (1908-2004)**

   Beginning her career with sales of creams made by her uncle, Estée formed her fortune in the manufacturing of cosmetic and beauty products. She owned an array of businesses under Estee Lauder Companies with a huge share in the cosmetic markets.

4. **Mary Kay Ash (1918 - 2001)**

   Experience of being a salesperson, motivated and aided Mary to build the empire of 'Mary Kay Cosmetics Inc.' in 1963. Management skills, dedication and zeal to work bestowed her with achievements like the Most Outstanding Woman in Business in the 20th Century reward by Lifetime Television. Her book Mary Kay on People Management is included in business courses at the Harvard Business School.

5. **Lillian Vernon (1929)**

   Born in Germany, she started working at home at 22 and rose it to be the first female-owned company to be listed on the American Stock Exchange. Today, 'Lillian Vernon Corporation' is one of the country's leading catalog retailers.

6. **Martha Stewart (1941)**

Commonly known as 'Lifestyle Guru', Martha initially appeared in fashion shows and advertisements. Later she ventured into the catering business and transformed it into 'Martha Stewart Living Omni media, Inc.,' her company is involved with publications & broadcasting, e-commerce as well as lifestyle products.

7. **Anita Roddick (1943 - 2007)**

After experimenting in various traits, Anita kicked off 'The Body Shop' initially to support her family. Her environment friendly products made from natural ingredients, packaged in recyclable materials grabbed her immense business growth and numerous rewards. She demonstrated that businesses can act as social campaign for worthy causes.

8. **Vera Wang (1949)**

A designer known for her bridal wear, Vera was a senior fashion editor for Vogue. She also worked at Ralph Lauren as a design director before stepping out to set her own studio. Her work in designing sports costumes and less expensive line of ready-to-wear clothing called Very Vera is also highly appreciated.

9. **Oprah Winfrey (1954)**

A media giant, Oprah ruled the American media as a talk-show host, an actress as well as a producer. This philanthropist and a co-author spun off Oxygen Media, operating a cable television network for women. She also supported Barack Obama for presidency and shows interest in politics.

10. **Debbi Fields (1956)**

This proud owner of 'Mrs. Fields Bakeries' proved that a multimillion dollar enterprise can be built on something as simple as baking a cookie. Often referred as 'the tough cookie', Debbi also is an author of several cookbooks.

9

Female Labour Participation in Rural and Urban India: Does Housewives' Work Count?

Labour force participation in India responds to economic, social, cultural and demographic mechanisms

Employment, unemployment, and unpaid labour were all measured in the 1999/2000 Indian National Sample Survey. Men's official labour force participation stood at 85% and women's at 35%. The overall rate of labour force participation among women had fallen since 1989. Furthermore, measurement issues create doubt about the real rates of change of women's self-employment. Women's domestic and farming work can sometimes arguably be classified as self-employment. However many women instead report themselves as housewives. The statistics reveal a U curve of female employment by education levels. A detailed measurement of both domestic work and other unpaid work is provided. Women in the Muslim cultural group do more extra-domestic work than women in other cultural groups.

Economic poverty causes employment to be more likely. We provide a number of reasons which help explain both the work patterns and the housewifisation pattern. These include both subjective factors as well as economic and demographic factors.

Introduction

In India, as elsewhere, people face a conflict over time spent on housework and childcare versus time spent on paid work. Ironically, if people are paid market rates for childcare and cooking work, rather high valuations are put on these supposedly 'domestic' tasks. Some estimates of the national income have been made which adjust for the unpaid unmarketised domestic work in the USA. These show large increases in the Gross Domestic Product. However, since the work is actually not monetised, people in general don't normatively accord 'domestic work' the values imputed in such studies. Instead, they devalue this work and many people consider it to be women's work. In India, across a variety of regional and cultural divisions, domestic work and childcare are widely considered to be women's work. It is often implicitly seen as undignified for a man to actually get involved in the dirty work of child cleaning, the messy work of dishwashing, or the time consuming women's jobs of cooking curries or sweeping the floors. Cleaning toilets is universally women's work and the conditions in which some dalit people work as toilet attenders are unbelievably unsanitary and unpleasant.

The unpleasant aspects of domestic work were analyzed by Thorstein Veblen who is better known for his theory of the leisure class. Veblen argued that the dominant people in the leisure class would visibly display time-wasting behaviours whilst they depend on the devoted or enslaved work of others who would do all the essential services such as cooking, cleaning, and clearing away. Veblen argued that by showing themselves to be cleaner than the working classes, both feudal and capitalist ruling classes displayed their prowess and status. Their physical prowess during military times was augmented by their considerable personal autonomy and control over other people's bodily movements even in peacetime. Veblen is famous for the theory of conspicuous consumption in which even the middle classes were found to emulate the lazy and excessively luxurious behaviours of the rich.

Why do middle classes do this? In part, it is because emulating the behaviours demonstrates one's identification with the higher class. This identification can have subtle cheering effects on someone who is actually oppressed within a hierarchy but prefers to imagine that they are not too far down that hierarchy.

This paper examines women's work in India and how huge swathes of women are devoted only to unremunerated work. By contrast, being unemployed is rather rare among men. For women, the orthodox indicators of unemployment do not really apply. Instead it is non-employment time that we need to focus upon. In India the National Sample Survey Organisation (NSSO) has repeatedly given measures of women's time spent on a variety of activities which broadly one can call the informal sector. These measures are, however, provided if and only if the woman first declares that she has no paid work, is not unemployed per se, and is doing domestic work only. She cannot declare herself self-employed either so the category of 'housewives' is an appropriate label for this residual group of non-employed women who were asked the questions about unremunerated work.

We provide details of this survey and a summary of the findings in this paper. We conclude with a normative discussion of the situation.

The more women's time is allocated to paid employment, the less of their time is available for the unpaid work. Most western feminists would argue that the unpaid work done by women tends to get too little attention, and that its social and economic valuation is unreasonably low. Yet they do not go so far as to hope for an increase in the time spent on domestic work. The main issue, they would argue, is the rewards and conditions of the work, both domestic and paid work. Women should be autonomous (Jejeebhoy and Sathar), they should be paid appropriate rates for paid work and they should not be oppressed or coerced in their economic decisions. Ironically, however, most housewives will quickly argue that they 'chose' to be housewives and 'not to work'.

This reaction reflects a revaluation in which the woman positively values her role in the family and prefers not to engage in some other set of more public roles.

As indicated by these field data, there is a delicately balanced set of normative principles lying behind all the decisions people make about labouring. Even when we describe labouring, we unintentionally invoke or hint at some of these norms. In this paper we tread a fine line between positive and normative description. In a sense we integrate positive description with normative analysis. We take 'labouring' and 'working' to mean the same thing, whilst 'employment' refers to the narrower subset of paid work.

The International Labour Office (ILO) defines unemployment in a rather open way, requiring that the person be seeking work and also be available for work during the two weeks preceding the interview. For women who are doing child care, it is hard to claim that they are really seeking work even if the woman would, in some hypothetical sense, perhaps be willing to be employed if she could.

In the villages where Olsen did fieldwork in 1995-6, groups of very poor women had created a village level crèche and this had enabled a number of the women to do more paid work. This showed that they had been unemployed previously, due to child care duties.

However in ILO terms, they couldn't have claimed to be unemployed because the child care work kept them from actually seeking work. Andhra Pradesh where the fieldwork occurred has one of the highest female labour force participation rates of all the large Indian states. Details are given in a separate paper available from the authors.

The ILO's definition of labour-market inactivity has been changing over time since 1970 and it now tends to include less of the family helpers as 'inactive'. The unpaid family helper nowadays tends to be classified as a contributing family worker. In this way there is a drift toward higher recorded labour-force participation of women and children even though this does not necessarily correspond to a real change or increase in their working hours.

Most importantly, the frame of reference of this paper considers labour relations – including employment, class and gender relations – to lie behind all outcomes that are measured for groups of individuals in India's large-scale national surveys. We step back from making judgements about which forms of labouring are desirable or otherwise. We describe the tendencies that are currently causing people to do paid work in the Indian economy and, in particular, we examine the tendency to be labour-market 'inactive' in detail.

Both men's and women's labour force involvements are explored here with a view to a balanced, nuanced and in-depth analysis of the differences that emerge between groups of people. These differences have several meanings. Firstly, they imply that causal tendencies are operating concurrently on fairly big homogeneous groups of people. Shared features of the groups include economic poverty, cultural background, health, and demographic conditions.

Secondly, homogenous groups may imply that a majority of people of one type make a similar explicit choice, e.g. one group avoids paid work and tends to do domestic work. This interpretation of domestic work seems to sound rather innocuous and structuralism. But the career break often has negative effects on a person's lifetime chances in the labour market. Constraints and constraining social norms can lead to such "choices" actually being sub-optimal or disempowering for the individual argues that women are exploited through the capitalist system in particular. They do socially necessary labour which was normally not allowed for even in Marxist theorizations of the reserve army of labour. Thirdly, the differences between groups suggest that policy made with one image of 'women's needs' may go wrong if applied to all women.

Extending a gender analysis to allow for men's needs suggests further nuances: For instance, in India, are employers expecting to pay a breadwinner's wage to each man? Do employed women therefore get a lower wage than men for subjective reasons? One paper cannot answer all these questions but we do succeed in describing the overall situation in terms of employment outcomes in some detail.

Work in India is predominantly conducted outside of paid formal employment contracts. There is a huge formal sector in urban areas, but both rural and urban India also has large numbers of people doing farming, trading and other work in informal enterprises. Instead a range of remuneration arrangements for farmers, traders, other proprietors and their families, non-family helpers, and piece-rate workers cause low employment participation rates. Among women there was a long-term downward trend in the labour-force participation rates 1901-1971. This long-term trend reflected the growth of the distinct role of the housewife over the period 1901-1971 and was unfortunately associated with a rising male sex ratio in the population as a whole. This appearance of lower women's participation was further exaggerated by some changes in the recording of employment in the 1971 Census. The Census of that year was hard to compare with previous years.

Since 1971 there has been a stabilization of women's employment.

The ILO database www.laborsta.org shows no rise in women's economic activity rates for India 1972-2002.1 These data show 31% of women working in 1970, 31% in 1980, 27% in 1990, and 30% for India in 2000. In other words there is no substantial change, according to this source.

The measures of work participation obtained by the National Council for Agro-Economic Research (NCAER) in their survey in 1997 showed labour force participation rates of 52% among men and 26% among women. Their calculations used both usual and subsidiary status. The usual status refers to someone having six months per year or more of paid work or self employment. For those who do not have that regularity of work, the presence of any paid work can then be considered to give a 'subsidiary' status of participating. Mainly women were brought into the records via this subsidiary working status. At the all-India level it raised women's labour force participation from 18 to 26%. The NCAER figures closely mimic the Indian Census figures for 1991. The Census showed 27% of women and 53% of men were in the labour force using the combination of usual and subsidiary status. NCAER labels these figures clearly as 'work participation rates' indicating that inactivity, domestic work, and extra domestic work don't count as work.

Furthermore state differences in work participation rates are given using NCAER data. The change in female work participation rates due to including subsidiary status has different effects for different states. For those with low participation rates under the heading of 'usual' status there is a huge difference. Adding subsidiary workers in some cases doubles the work participation rate, e.g. from 9 to 29% in the Punjab, and a similarly large jump occurs in Uttar Pradesh.

The ILO presents for each five-year period its 'Projections and Estimates of female economic activity rate', also found in the UN Common Data Base as variable code 4270, dated on 5-year period centres. The gender differential in participation persists over time, but whether it is narrowing or not is an open question.

This paper is mainly cross-sectional. There is a strong tendency to be employed among all degree level graduates, including Muslim women. A U-curve of employment probabilities exists over education levels. This U curve is stronger among Muslim women than among other women due to a range of factors. These factors include the expectation (among certain families) that being seen in public could damage a woman's role as protector of the honour of her family; a sense that a woman's education is a way to gain social status and not just future wages; and a sense among household members that they can afford to enable one woman to stay at home most of the time – especially if the household is urban and middle income.

Among rural households, it is widely believed that it is prestigious for a Hindu woman to cook and serve food to her family and any guests that may come. In rural areas for these women to do domestic work only and nothing else is relatively rare. Instead, doing a range of paid and unpaid work, including some tasks that we call 'extra-domestic work', is more common. The tendency of naming a woman as being overall a housewife is very popular. A high status is generally associated with the role of housewife in parts of the country that have implicit cultural values associated with Sanskritisation, Brahmanical gender norms, and/or the habit of observing purdah. Because of the popularity of calling a woman a housewife, we have avoided using the 'principal status' of the person over a whole year and instead have focused upon each person's work during a one-week recall period. We use last week's work status as the main indicator of a person's employment status. Otherwise women's work would be understated as people try to exaggerate the presence of a housewife in each household.

The causal mechanisms behind the 'housewifery' pattern are explained and explored in the interpretive sections that complete the paper.

The 'principal' status is a generalisation derived in the field by NSS staff with respondents. It is not the same as the 'usual' status but is closely allied to it. NSS documents the subjective judgments that should be made in deriving the 'principal' status and derives the decision from the overview of the past year's work (via unrecorded recall). We begin with a brief review of literature, then introduce the large scale data set used in the paper, and finally present the results. The interpretation that takes up the last section follows retroductive logic: what social and cultural mechanisms must or may be operating to create the overall patterns that were observed in the data?

Review of Literature on Women's Labour Force Participation in India

The relevant literature includes economic theory, institutionalist revisions, gender and development theory, and some additional themes from demography and geography. In the literature on labour-force participation, standard sources begin with the supply of labour and quickly move on to mention human capital aspects of labour supply. According to this view, 34% of adult Indians participated in the labour market in 1991, and this figure comprised 16% among women and 51% among men. More up-to-date figures show a small decline in both women's and men's labour-force participation between 1993-94 and 1999-2000. 30% of the women in rural areas were working, as recorded in the National

Sample Survey of India using a combination of principal and subsidiary employment status, compared with 53% of men. Only 14% of urban women were working, by this measure. Detailed differences in the recall method of record-keeping imply that the two sources are not directly comparable. Mathur used the Indian Census 1991 data.

Sarvekshana shows a declining female labour force participation rate when comparing 1993/4 and 1999/00 using NSS. Jacob studied four different measures. The weekly and daily status measures of employment status showed the same overall trend. Specifically, over this period using NSS data the rural percentage in the labour force fell by 10% among women and by 4% among men. The urban percentage in the labour force fell 11% among women and there was no change among men. Basing his statistical analysis upon district-level Census data for 1991, Mathur used averages at the district level to model the 'response' of employment to education levels. A U curve can be seen using Mathur's data, among women since participation first falls between the illiterate group and the next group. Participation rises rapidly after that. Apart from updating the definitive study by Mathur, the present work admits more possibilities into the 'participation' category. Mathur allowed all main farmers, casual labour and employers to be grouped into the active group, following the Indian Census categories, but we add to this various home workers and family labour. In this way we obtain a variant on the labour-force participation rate that is consistent with current ILO definitions.

The human capital theory primarily predicts that wages reflect the rewards earned by human capital in productive enterprises. It has three parts however. First there is the potential worker's subjective reckoning of what they would earn if they worked for pay; secondly there is the act of gaining more education or training (which occurs both at schools and in firms); and third there is the reward firms give to productivity. This complex of factors has been unpicked carefully by other authors, who note that each stage faces certain problems. Basically the theory only relates crudely and roughly to reality. Firstly, it is not a person who reckons on earnings that they could make, it is a complex and yet cooperative household which can have one or several bargaining and decision-making processes going on. Secondly, investments in education and training are not merely individual rational choices but are also socially embedded decisions. Fevre has stressed the habitus component in which status gains, family enculturation, emulation of role models, and avoidance of stress all play a part. Thirdly, the rewards firms give to education have been shown to differ substantially across countries, regions, sectors, and by sex of worker. Deshpande argue that the gender pay gap observed in urban India occurs because gender-based discrimination is universal and enduring. Those women are overcrowded in low-paid, dead-end, and insecure and in short, "bad" jobs are easily verified. Kingdon insists on detailed evidence for such claims since the situation varies from place to place and from job to job.

These vagaries of human capital theory leave it wounded but not dead. The theory helps to show that there is an opportunity cost of avoiding labour-force participation. If the individual's returns to working are low, their opportunity cost of not working will be low too. They will then tend toward being labour-market inactive. If they have a degree, the opportunity cost is high since their workplace productivity is likely to be reckoned to be high. From human capital theory, one would expect an upward tendency in the labour force participation rate as we move across education levels.

Human capital theory is part of a wide-ranging neoclassical theory of labour supply and demand. Neoclassical theorists argue that supply and demand cause the wage to reward workers according to marginal productivity. Huge gender pay gaps exist.

These ranged in 1994 from 43% among illiterate and lower primary workers to 23% among graduates, averaging at 20% overall. A neoclassical economist would tend to argue that only market imperfections such as stereotypes, rigid segmentation by gender and cultural taboos on one sex doing certain operations can be introduced as explanatory factors. To a neoclassical economist, these factors are givens; they act as preferences of individuals; they are not part of the scope of economic science; and they cannot be treated in economic models.

The approach taken here is that the human capital claims can be augmented with a rich array of other claims arising in disciplines close to economics. The neoclassical approach is not necessarily the one that must lead the analysis. Statistical analysis was followed by reproduction – asking why these results came out – and then has been iterated with further statistical and qualitative analysis. The qualitative analysis uses both secondary reports and primary research.

The reason for jettisoning the neoclassical framework as a whole, whilst retaining some of its human capital claims, is that in rural and less-developed country contexts it has become abundantly clear that an individualistic framework is inadequate. Among economists, the "new home economics" evolved to handle this problem.

According to NHE, the result of the utility-maximizing decision at household level is thought to be an optimal distribution of the workers' efforts toward paid and unpaid work, and leisure.

Detailed research by Skoufias has uncovered patterns in India which are consistent with this theory. Skoufias' detailed study of seasonal movements in wages and work-time (spent working on farms, either paid or unpaid) concluded that women's labour time is seasonally spread quite differently from men's in India. This generalisation is also supported by older data, but in recent years women have taken on much more of the agricultural work than in the past. Certain tasks are taboo for women in most of rural India, notably plowing the land, but in general a feminisation of agricultural labour has occurred whilst men have tended to take most of the new non-agricultural jobs in rural areas.

Avoiding the whole neoclassical theoretical edifice, we can use political-economy institutionalism as hinted at by Ott and as spelt out in detail by Toye, Hodgson, and Harriss White. Veblen is one of the famous originators of today's institutionalism and several associations promote this as a new way to do pluralist economics.3 Institutionalism refers to an assumption that social norms are in a state of flux as they interact with rules and with personal interpretations that either reproduce those rules or change them. Institutions are never simply given. In the case of India's labour markets, for instance, there are institutionalised norms about the terms of employment. These help to define what people expect from "piecework" "group contracts" "daily casual labour", "exchange labour" and salaried work. Since norms are ever-changing, they are always potentially renegotiable and institutions are also differentiated even within one community (e.g. as we see with marriage and cohabitation occurring side by side in the West).

The European Association for Evolutionary Political Economy; the International Network for Economic Method; the Association for Heterodox Economics; and the IDEA network for development economists are four of these associations. Each has a website and publications. Institutionalist empirically studying the Indian labour market falls into three main types. First there are the women-in-development specialists, who focus on gender differentiation. Second there are studies of discrimination against women and its causes. Thirdly there are those who have examined the formation of labour gangs, neighbourhood work groups, trade unions, and bonded labour relationships, migrant labour and different types of work contracts.

All these three groups are pluralist; it is primarily economists who isolate their arguments away from the details of competing theories.

Specific authors working in the above areas include the following.

Firstly those who describe women's movement into active and visible self-employment indicate that it is perceived as highly desirable among these women for them to validate their work by calling it micro-enterprise or a business. The economic activity of women as a special group is the focus of Gautam and Tripathi in their description of women managing goats. Gulati notes that women's economic and commercial activity in India is restricted by ongoing expectations that they will still also meet a wide range of family expectations.

These difficulties, which women face in different ways, vary depending on whether they live as a daughter in the natal home, or as a wife in the marital home, or independently. Whilst there is some state variation, notably in the far north and east of India where non Hindu tribes are more predominant, there is considerable bias against women which links up labour-force inactivity with poor health and low education. Narasimhan goes onward to argue in favour of women organizing themselves separately from men in order to resist patriarchy.

Deshpande and Deshpande argue that human capital theory explains why the gender pay gap observed in urban India is a vicious circle:

'Asked why women invest less in their education and training, [economists] turn to the sexual division of labour which ascribes to women the role of housekeeper and to men that of the breadwinner. The sexual division of labour weakens women's commitment to the labour market but it maximizes the welfare of the household.

With their weak commitment, they choose, quite rationally, not to accumulate as much human capital as men do.'

However, Deshpande and Deshpande's own data show that urban women working in the service industries earn as much or more than men of the same educational level if that level is secondary school, and that the gender pay gap falls as education rises.

Therefore the bald statements that are sometimes made, as illustrated above, need perhaps to be carefully reconsidered in the light of detailed evidence. Our further research will take up the wage-rate question in detail but so far we are just looking at work participation rates. Kapadia looked closely at rural labouring and finds that women as well as men often form labour gangs in order to increase their bargaining power vis a vis the employers of casual labour. Interviews by Davuluri Venkateswarlu also show that women join contracting groups to do casual labour, preferring that to domestic labour and unpaid labour. DaCorta and Venkateswarlu argue that the feminisation of the rural agricultural labour force is not necessarily good for women but it is a strong trend.

The variety of labouring contracts has been described in detail by Breman with respect to migrant labour and by Rogaly with respect to field labouring in north India. The bargaining power of the worker is influenced by a whole range of factors which critically affect the wage struck each day. Rogaly is one of the few researchers to have explored this phenomenon although Agarwal has theorized it with regard to women's work choices. A bargaining approach to the evolution of the gender pay gap might be a rich way of challenging neoclassical theory with a substantive alternative.

Thus a rich arena of social relations linked with power-rich hierarchies has been explored by this pluralist, multi-disciplinary authors studying the work economy. All of these institutionalist have paid due attention to unpaid work. Few of them have offered any large-scale statistical evidence. Many institutionalist studies rest upon a locally based case-study dataset because that is how the terms and conditions of specific labouring contracts are best examined. This paper tries to fill the gap whilst being sensitive to the claims made by the women-in-development school in particular.

Authors from another theoretical orientation, the "gender and development" school have argued that households have cultures, households engage in social class relations, and households experience both bargaining and cooperation among their members. The gender and development school differs from the women-in-development school in that class and gender are seen as interacting. Women are not simply seen as a homogenous group.

GAD and WID are sometimes posed as opposites, but GAD builds upon the insights of WID for a GAD analysis of the right to work in India.

The use of statistical evidence to back up these theories has been prominent in the work of Dreze and Sen, Swaminathan, Agarwal, and Srivastava. These authors attribute the terrible overall outcomes experienced by Indian women due to patriarchal and exploitative capitalist culture. Other than those mentioned here, however, most feminists in India have tended to avoid statistics. In the interests of bridging the chasm between neoclassical economists and some feminists, our methodological pluralist research aims to mediate between schools of thought such as NHE vs. GAD.

When labour-force involvement is classified into employment, self employment, unpaid family labour, inactivity, and other, we effectively study the labour-force involvement in a reductionist way at the 'individual' unit of analysis. A Marxist view on this augments both GAD and NHE by studying inter-household farm exploitation. Byres and other Marxists have argued that resources owned at household level under the current legal system must be taken into account. In this paper we have allowed for the social class system which is an open system of inter-household employment relationships. In regressions we use land owned, indicators based on employment, and indicators of tenancy and poverty. Self-employment itself is a class outcome which acts as a dependent variable.

Our pluralist approach also included three further hypotheses arising from demographers, the anthropological study of dowry, in which boys' families receive and girls' families give large amounts in cash and in kind, and studies of girls' lower education rates. A separate paper uses regression to draw out the U curve of housewifisation while controlling for all these important factors. Variables which were controlled for included the number of children in the household, the age of the respondent, allowing curvature and dummies for India's states to have state-wise differentiation in labour markets for a variety of agro-climatic and historical/institutional reasons.

The cross-tabulations and Figures in this paper arise from gross averages but they are consistent with the regression equations. It would be ideal to allow for minor work-relevant health differences among the population too. In the UK where 20% of the adult population has a disability of some kind affecting their ability to work, labour-force participation studies routinely control for ill health. However in India's National Sample Survey 55th round there is no indicator of temporary or mild disability. Instead there is a mutually exclusive status known as 'unable to work due to disability'. Such people are simply grouped here into the inactive category. There was no question on 'long-term limiting illnesses as found in Western surveys.

Caste differences and the various religious groupings were found to have significant association with work outcomes in India. Important aspects of caste are experienced at the 'upper' end of the spectrum in the differences between Brahman and other 'forward' castes such as the Merchants and the Reddy farming castes.

The upper castes are highly differentiated over space, and no records are kept of the specific castes in NSS of the detailed caste name of households.

Analysis of caste in the detailed sense in which it is lived therefore has to occur within a more detailed, triangulated study. Table 1 shows the evidence for main caste groups that is available from NSS 55th round. For details of one fieldwork site in Andhra Pradesh in 1986-87 and 1995 and the ESRC Data Set Study Number 3927. There it was found that the labour relations of merchant castes were particularly strongly gendered, since their womenfolk rarely if ever worked for anyone else. Brahmin women, too, rarely worked for pay at all and was rarely seen in the fields. However among the middle and lower castes and among Muslim people who were 15% of the local population work for pay was common for both men and women. The detailed study of caste allows occupational patterns to emerge as linked to small scale caste groups, such as Kshatriya and Chetties as well as Kummaaris, who are often small farmers as well as potters, Aacharyas, and so on. For a brief review of gendered aspects of caste and labouring see Raghuram.

Data and Methodology

In our analysis, labour-force involvements are classified as follows: Employed; self-employed, which includes own account workers and unpaid family labour; unemployed; and inactive. The last category covers 'attending to domestic duties' as well as student, retired, ill and other. Table 1 shows the percentages of the Indian working-age population falling into these categories in 1994. We used ages 16-65 although, in addition, many Indian children also work. For those adults who do domestic work, two collapsed categories are shown here. Details of the recording of extra-domestic work are in Appendix 1, and the results are summarized in Tables 3 and 4. In the NSS in 1994, a few men aged 16-65 were doing domestic work (about 1% -- but many more if the over-65s were included). However in 1999 no men were recorded as such. This step backward in the social construction of housewifery and is unnecessary since many men are labour-market inactive and some of them do informal-sector work. It would be ideal to return to a more sex-blind recording of the employment statuses.

Traditionally gender theorists have stressed that work in the informal sector should probably appear as 'self-employed', which is possible if the household's respondent argues that that is the best way of categorizing a person. For many women, and a few men, 'attending to domestic duties' was the main employment status, but there was nevertheless performance of a wide range of up to 12 activities which would, by many people, be considered to be productive and 'in' the labour market. These are not remunerated activities, but they contribute to the household's livelihood. In the questionnaire, the wording specifies that the person 'attended domestic duties and also engaged in free collection of goods, sewing, tailoring, weaving, etc. for household use.' The activities that are considered here as 'extra-domestic' are:

- husking paddy;
- grinding grain;
- preparing sugar for home use;
- preserving meat or fish;
- collecting firewood or dung;
- making cow-dung cakes for the fire;
- kitchen garden or orchard maintenance;
- work in poultry/dairy;
- fish, small game, fruits or vegetable gathering;
- making baskets or mats;
- sewing, tailoring, weaving;
- Tutoring of own or others' children free of charge.

These activities were grouped under the headings 'food preparation work', 'fuel and fire work', and 'informal sector unpaid work', respectively, in Table 5. Jacob shows that 26% of the urban female domestic workers did 'sewing, tailoring, etc.'

13% of urban female domestic workers did 'tutoring of own children', and 9% of the urban and 36% of the rural female domestic workers worked in a kitchen garden, did poultry work, or similar. Overall, urban women were more likely to be working purely as housewives than were rural women. This pattern may support Mies's claim that modernization would imply a growing housewifisation.

Further details about the survey form the rest of this section. General Introduction to NSS 55th Round

The National Sample Survey is an integrated survey on household consumer expenditure, employment, unemployment and informal non-agricultural work. It covers both individuals' work and household principal occupation.

Detailed indicators of people's personal principal and subsidiary occupation, hours worked, and earnings are provided. At the household level, income estimates are not provided. Instead, the wealth/poverty spectrum is measured using household-level percapita expenditure. This indicator is not very sophisticated but it does allow the relative spending of households to be taken into consideration.

Sampling

The NSS has used a sampling scheme that rotates on the calendar months for its Central samples. Thus all quarters of one calendar year are represented in all regions. The survey period of the 55th Round is 1st July, 1999 to 30th June, 2000. A sample of 10,400 first-stage units was surveyed at all-India level.

In addition to these main 10,400 fsus, which are known as the Central sample, there are state samples with additional fsu's. All the States/ Union Territories except for Andaman & Nicobar

Islands, Dadra & Nagar Haveli and Lakhshadweep participated in the 55th round at least on an equal matching basis compared to the size of the central sample. The state samples did not have the rotating timing found in the central sample. The rotation is useful because it means that when a one-week recall period is used, at least half the overall samples are spread out over the entire year. In this paper, both the central sample and state samples have been used together to maximize the sample size. 360,000 people aged 16-65, and 592,000 aged 0 to 99 years were in the survey. The average household size was 5.8 and there were on average 2 children under the age of 16. Results: Indian Women's Labour Force

Participation

In Tables 1 and 2 the overall level of labour-force participation is seen to be 85% among men and 35% among women using the one week recall method. In the National Human Development Report 2001, published by the Planning Commission in 2002, the same NSS data are used to report the labour-force participation rates as they were recorded at three time-points: 1989, 1994, and 1999-2000. The rates shown there for 1999-2000 are very similar to our estimates: 84% among men and 39% among women. Here the combination "usual principal and subsidiary status or seeking or available for work" was used. Thus, whether one uses one-week recall or the usual and-subsidiary combination, the results are nearly the same.

Going back in time, this Report shows both participation rates declining, with men's rates falling from 87% in 1983 to 84% in 1999-2000. Women's rates fell from 44% in 1983 to 39% in 1999-2000 – a larger decline on a smaller base.

The meanings of this decline are multiple depending on one's policy perspective. Some of the important meanings of withdrawing women from employment are positively valued by many Indian residents quite apart from the commercial effects.

In Table 2 it can be seen that self-employment is a more important category of work among men than among women. However, as stressed in the National Human Development Report, the rates of participation differ depending on which social category the person is in. In the rest of our discussion we will focus on some of the diversity within India's overall averages.

As shown in Table 4, women's employment rates fall as caste status rises. It is also notable that rural and urban employment rates are very different. In both places however women do plenty of self-employment. In rural areas this is mostly agricultural whereas in urban areas it is mainly informal-sector and small-scale manufacturing.

The U curve of employment per se is shown in Figure 1. A logistic regression of employment per se also showed that the tendency to have a job (including casual work) first falls with education moving from illiteracy toward middle levels, and then rises. In other words both net and gross patterns showed a U curve. The rapid decline in rates of inactivity among both Hindu and Muslim women as they reach graduate status can be seen in Figure 1. Both Hindu and Muslim women tend to have a typical inverted U of labour-force participation over age-groups. Hindu and Muslim women's rates of labour force participation are different across a wide spectrum of education levels excepting among graduates. We can test for the differences for other major religions, as done also in the National Human Development Report, but we would do this only in the context of detailed evidence about each religious grouping. Since we know most about Hindu and Muslim cultural groupings, we have only described these two in Figure 3.

The education effects found in the regression indicated only weak support for the human capital theory of labour supply. The rise in labour supply only applied when we compared highly educated women to those in the middle levels of education. Below that there is an apparent perversity. Women of low education levels are more likely to work than those of middle levels. The causal mechanism behind this is a nexus of household-level poverty. We allowed for this in the regression by using a dummy variable for being in a poor household. Poor women are most likely to take casual paid work. Many Indians perceive poor women's employment as being a response to their household income crisis. It is seen as necessary drudgery for them from which housewives have been relieved. The regression equation allowed for much more than education.

Institutional factors were present and statistically significant. The different states' cultural, regulatory and historical backgrounds were allowed for by using state dummies, many of which were highly significant.

Poverty and Labour Market Outcomes Household level economic poverty was measured by the NSS by getting item-wise recall of monthly expenditure and then adjusting this for the household size, giving a per capita indicator. Those people living in households with less than half of the median monthly expenditure were deemed to be poor for the purposes of the simple regressions here. Such an analysis omits intrahousehold differentials in the control over expenditure, noneconomic aspects of poverty, and differentials in the cost of different types of people. Because they use a recall method, the accuracy of the figures for household economic poverty is further cast into doubt. This paper uses the indicator of household economic poverty in a rough and ready fashion because of these caveats.

Poverty (in this sense) is far more prevalent among the rural scheduled castes and scheduled tribes than in other parts of the population. In this way and others, these regression results suffer from endogeneity. The same causal mechanisms that are represented by one variable are also to some extent embedded in other variables. Economic poverty, for instance, is measured directly but then is also proxied by some other variables.

Landholding is represented both by the owned holding and the operational landholding. These endogeneities are not too problematic if we take the regression for what it is: a description of the outcomes of a complex array of causal mechanisms which work both actually and counterfactually. They operate not only in their own right, but also only in contexts in which they are able to have effects. We cannot expect regression to simply separate all the causal mechanisms since the operationalizations of social causes are fraught with overlaps between context and specific causes.

We find that people whose work as tenant farmers are less likely to be employed and more likely to be self-employed themselves.

We also find that poor households have a reduced tendency to have a woman working purely within the home, because the women in these households tend to go out for employment. Many of these poor women have a double burden of domestic and paid work or even a triple burden of domestic, farming and paid work. A third warranted argument is much more controversial. Those households which pull themselves out of poverty are more likely to withdraw the woman from the labour market. Women's withdrawal from employment can be an elegant yet silent testimony to the couple's economic success.

Village level fieldwork in Andhra Pradesh helped Olsen to learn that having a woman kept in private is a prestigious and high-status form of invisibility. Many housewives are discouraged from riding bikes even though most learn to ride during their childhood. In a sense most Indian women observe a form of purdah. These patterns cut across castes and religious groupings. The irony of the high-status women who are often being made invisible via social norms only increases the social distance between them and the poor or low status women. The norms for different groups of women are quite different and so what a woman 'chooses' is couched in her specific context, her economic / political / caste / religion / lineage and locality as well as her marital status and whether she has borne children. Because of this differentiation it is dangerous to generalize.

Interpretation of Cultural Factors

Qualitative research helps in exploring the meanings people attach to women doing domestic work. Across India there is a broad cultural tendency to 'Hinduisation', such that even among India's Muslims and other minorities some cultural patterns mimic those of the dominant Hindu groups. These include dowry, patrilocality, and arranged marriages for instance. Agarwal's review of inheritance by widows goes so far as to ignore all minority ST and Muslim groups, using only Hinduism-based examples and sources, which is perhaps unfortunate, but does reflect the widespread understanding that the gender order is of a nearly nation-wide nature and is not simply or solely embedded in religious groupings and civil law.

Agarwal's work crosses over between WID, GAD, institutionalism and cultural studies, because she has studied both the dynamics of household bargaining and the roles of religious difference and state-wise policy differentiation across the four countries of South Asia. The delicate interplay of culture and local social norms leads to about five aspects of housewifery roles which are often perceived to be positively valued. These include: -

- 'Sanskritisation' a process of displaying upward mobility by invoking and demonstrating honourable roles for women , e.g. as the provider of refreshments at functions, the calm manager of the household, and the beautiful object of admiration.
- Even women who have professional occupations can successfully continue with their housewifery roles by

employing other women to do much of the nitty gritty daily work so there is no problem with the double burden.

- Women can take care of these matters without involving their employed men folk. Men's long working hours support the full domestic responsibilities falling upon mothers' and wives' shoulders at home. The exclusion of men from the role of housewife, and from all records of extra-domestic work in NSS 55th round, demonstrates a growing patriarchal role demarcation in India. It is widely seen as more dignified for men to be uninvolved with domestic matters.
- Women who do farming work can be seen as the helpmeet and unpaid worker of the male household head. This sexist and andocentric approach to farming households is a patriarchal value implicitly held vary widely in society. Finally,
- Many people prefer women to act submissive and deferential toward elders and toward men. Acting deferential is considered to be appropriate and to keep the women in safe relationship networks which protect the women in a patronizing way. These women insist that they have a large and valued 'private life'. However they are effectively then barred from engaging in public life.

To the extent that people hold these values they will intersubjectively create spaces in which middle-income women act as housewives.

The opponents of patriarchy are many and diverse, and their voice has been loudest among the academic authors already cited. They argue that deferential and excessively private roles are bad for women. By listing them, we enable readers to consider the pros and cons of the U curve situation rather systematically.

(1) Dependency of most wives on a male breadwinner and his family's property.

(2) Low bargaining power of women so that they cannot easily exit, or threaten to exit, a marital home even if there is alcoholism, an affair, or domestic violence.
(3) The woman who has neither job nor self-employment can, at times, be isolated and lose confidence.
(4) Poor educational outcomes of girls.
(5) Women fall behind in their knowledge of their own profession or occupation.
(6) Ultimately in this context women are often seen in a diminutive, degraded, and denigrated light. Their work is seen as 'helping' work even if it would be classified as 'employment' or 'self-employment' if done by a man.
(7) Women who are not in relationships are seen as exceptional, threatening, odd and often mentally unstable.
(8) Sexual harassment of working women goes hand in hand with the patronization of non-working women.
(9) The earnings of girls and women may be seen as 'pin money', as temporary, as nonessential.

Conclusion

The paper has described a complex situation in which a U curve of women's employment by education levels is caused by a mixture of economic and cultural factors. The whole paper is suffused with interdisciplinary pluralism so that these factors can be taken into account in a balanced way. So-called 'inactive' people can be divided into the inactive per se versus those who were recorded as doing some extra domestic work. The ILO definition of unemployment is not sufficiently detailed to help us clarify the nature of the borderline between employment and nonemployment. This borderline seems to be permeable and socially constructed.

The U curve was explored in some detail using statistical evidence.

The paper ended with a list of the felt advantages and disadvantages of women working as housewives – the typical scenario at the bottom of the U among middle-educated women.

The standard norms for housewives are adapted for poor women, who often have a double or triple burden of work, and for rich women who can employ others to assist them whilst still being the manager of a household. Great heterogeneity among women is therefore noted. One hopes that a diversification of values (especially about men and women doing domestic work) and a serious ethical discussion of the morality of patriarchy can be based on this kind of overview study. We cited many authors who have engaged in this serious discussion but we also note that the situation appears to be getting worse instead of better in India since its economic liberalization around 1991.

10

WOMEN AND MEN IN INDIA, 2011: HIGHLIGHTS

With a view to facilitating the availability of gender statistics at one place on a wide range of issues- violence against women, economic empowerment, leadership & participation, health, education and human rights, the Central Statistics Office (CSO), Government of India has been bringing out the publication "Women and Men in India" on a regular basis since 1995. CSO has endeavored to focus in this publication on such crucial statistical indicators of socio-economic relevance as are deemed best in portraying gender inequality, gender bias and gender discrimination.

Population and Vital Statistics

With 1176.74 million persons, India accounts for about 16% of world population in 2010. Seventy percent of the population lives in rural areas. Two important demographic goals of the National Population Policy (2000) are:

1. Achieving the population replacement level by 2010 and a stable population by 2045. TFR, which was 3.2 in 2000, has declined to 2.6 in 2008. Thus, India is moving towards its goal of replacement level fertility of 2.1.
2. The decadal growth of population during 1991-2001 was 21.5% which is projected to be 15.9% for 2001-2011.
3. The average annual exponential growth rate for men during 1991-2001 was 1.92% as against 1.99% for women. The total annual exponential growth rate for 2006-10 has been estimated at 1.95%.

4. The sex ratio was 933 in 2001 and is projected to be 932 in 2010.
5. Preference for son varies according to social groups and regions in India. 20% men and 22.3% women prefer to have more sons than daughters.
6. An increasing trend in mean age at marriage is observed for females in India. It has gone up from 19.8 years in 2000 to 20.7 years in 2008.
7. The Total Fertility Rate (TFR) is 2.6 for the year 2008, being 2.9 in the rural areas and 2.0 in the urban areas
8. The mortality rate among females across all ages is 6.8 and that among males is 8.0 for the year 2008. The female mortality rate in the age group 0-4 years has declined to 16.1 in 2008 from 20.6 in 2000.
9. Out of 150.18 million households in the rural areas in 2004-05, 16.67 million are Female Headed Households (11.10%). In the urban sector, out of the total of 56.97 million households, 4.85 million are Female Headed (10.9%).
10. The percentage of never married females and married females across all the age groups is 43.9 and 47.9, respectively, in 2008. The Widowed/ Divorced or Separated constitute 8.0% of the population in 2008
11. The migration percentage in different streams for females as per the Census 2001 is: rural to rural-71%; rural to urban-13.6%; urban to urban-9.7% and urban toRural-5.6%. The migration among females is due to marriage (64.9%). Among the males, the important cause of migration is employment (37.6%).

Health and Well Being

12. The majority of women go through their life in a state of nutritional stress- they are anemic and malnourished.

Poverty, early marriage, malnutrition and lack of health care during pregnancy are the major reasons for both maternal and infant mortality. The average Indian woman bears her first child before she is 22 years old, and has little control over her own fertility and reproductive health. In rural India, almost 60 per cent of girls are married before they are 13. Nearly 60 per cent of married girls bear children before they are 19. Almost one third of all babies are born with low birth weight.

14. Infant Mortality Rate (IMR) has been decreasing over the years. The IMR for females in India is 55 compared to 52 for males in 2008.
15. Life Expectancy at Birth (LEB) has increased more among women compared to men. It is observed that in 2002-06 LEB for males was 62.6 years compared to 64.2 years for females.
16. Delivery at a health facility is an indicator of programmatic effort for safe motherhood. It is observed that 47% deliveries took place at a health facility in India.
17. Maternal Mortality in India during 2004-06 is 254 per 100,000 live births, being the highest in Assam (485) followed by Uttar Pradesh (440) and Rajasthan (388). The percentage distribution of deaths of expected mothers due to causes related with pregnancy and child birth shows that hemorrhage is the most common cause (38%). Other causes are sepsis (11%), abortion (8%) and obstructed labour (5%).
18. 56% of the women in the age group 15-19 are anemic The share of deliveries in hospitals, maternity/ nursing homes, health centers, etc. is 40.8% while the deliveries assisted by doctors, trained 'dais', trained midwives, trained nurses, etc. constitute another 48.8%.
19. Over 99% of married women know about any of the methods of contraception. The awareness about the female

sterilization is very high in both urban and rural areas. The rural women are found to be less aware about the traditional methods (56.5%), though it has increased significantly over the last 7-8 years.

20. Women also lead a differential life style. 32% women in India drink alcohol, 57% chew paan masala and 33% women smoke currently.

Literacy and Education

20. Census of India, 2001 indicates that only 54% women are literate as compared to 76% men. Female literacy is highest in Kerala (88%) and lowest in Bihar (33%). The Adult Literacy rate of females is 48% in 2001 against 73.4% for adult males. However, 14.6% females and 17.4% males are literate without any formal education.
21. Year 2007-08 indicates a trend reversal; with the girls' enrolment in the three levels of school education – primary, middle and secondary – being more than that of boys in the respective levels. Girls' enrolment for the year 2007-08 in primary classes was 115.3%, 81.5% in middle school and 49.4% in high/ higher secondary classes. The year 2007-08 records 24.4% as the dropout rate for the girls in the primary classes and 57.3% for secondary showing marginal decline in dropout rates as compared to 2006-07.
22. The main reasons of females never attending school are 'expensive cost of education', 'not interested in studies', 'education is not considered necessary' and 'required for household work'.
23. In 2007-08, the number of girls enrolled in primary classes was 91 per 100 boys and for middle classes it was 84 girls per 100 boys. In the secondary section, the ratio stands at 77 girls per 100 boys. In the year 2006-07, there were 76.9 females per 100 males enrolled in arts stream in university education. For science, it was 71.2 females per 100 males

and in commerce, there were 60.9 females per 100 males. The engineering and technical education consisted of 35.8 females per 100 males and in medicine there were 89.5 females enrolled per 100 males.

24. In 2007-08, at primary and middle school level, there were 80 and 67 female teachers respectively per 100 male teachers. At the secondary school level, it was 61 female teachers per 100 male teachers.

Participation in Economy

25. As per Census 2001, the number of workers in the urban areas is 92.28 million of which only 16.10 million are females. In rural areas, out of 310 million workers, 111 million are females. 42.95% of the rural female working population is involved as agricultural labour. Women constitute 90 per cent of the total marginal workers of the country. As per NSS 64thRound, 2007-08, the workforce participation rate of females in rural sector was 28.9 while that for males was 54.8. In Urban sector, it was 13.8 for females and 55.4 for males. According to Quarterly Employment Review, Ministry of Labour, the total employment of women in organized sector was 19.5% in 2007.

26. Women work longer hours than men, and carry the major share of household and community work that is unpaid and invisible. According to the pilot Time Use Survey conducted in 18,620 households spread over six selected States, namely, Haryana, Madhya Pradesh, Gujarat, Orissa, Tamil Nadu and Meghalaya during the period June 1998 to July 1999, women spent about 2.1 hours per day on cooking food and about 1.1 hours on cleaning the households and utensils. Men's participation in these activities was nominal. Taking care of children was one of the major responsibilities of women, as they spent about 3.16 hours per week on these activities as compared to only 0.32 hours by males.

There were far fewer women in the paid workforce than there were men. There were more unemployed women than there were unemployed men.

27. It has been estimated that women's wage rates are, on the average, 75% of men's wage rates and constitute only one fourth of the family income. In no State do women and men earn equal wages in agriculture. Also, women generally work in the informal sector where wages are lower and they are not covered by labour laws. Women workers are also engaged in piecework and subcontracting at exploitative rates.
28. Women's contribution to agriculture — whether it be subsistence farming or commercial agriculture — when measured in terms of the number of tasks performed and time spent, is greater than men. Most of the work that women do, such as collecting fuel, fodder and water, or growing vegetables, or keeping poultry for domestic consumption, goes unrecorded in the Census counts.
29. The Public Sector consists of highest number of women in community, social and personal services, whereas in private sector majority of employed women are in manufacturing industries.
30. The Ministry of Rural Development runs various programmes to bring women into mainstream and to encourage their participation in the process of national development. These programmes have special components for women and funds are earmarked as 'Women Component'. The various schemes benefiting women are the Sampoorna Gramin Rozgar Yojana (SGRY), the Swarnjayanti Gram Swarozgar Yojana (SGSY), the Indira Awaas Yojana (IAY), Central Rural Sanitation Programme (CRSP), and the Accelerated Rural Water Supply Programme (ARWSP). The statistics of the Department of Rural Development state that in 2008-09, 18.61 lakh Swarojgaris were employed

out of which 64.80% were female beneficiaries. Percentage of women employed in NREGA has increased from 42.58 in 2007-08 to 47.88 in 2008-09.

30. The Basic Statistical Returns of Scheduled Commercial Banks in India, 2008 finds that in rural areas only 2.79% of female employees are officers, 7.04% are clerks and 5.19% are subordinates. In semi-urban areas, these figures are 7.01%, 16.7% and 9.22%, respectively, whereas in urban areas the officers, clerks and subordinates are 14.07%, 27.7% and 10.58% respectively

31. Also, 21% bank accounts in commercial banks belong to females. The share (in terms of amounts deposited) of females in total deposited amount is 10.3%.

Participation in Decision-making

32. Although Indian women played a major role in the freedom movement, it did not translate into continued participation in public life in the post-independence era. On the contrary, many women withdrew into their homes, secure in the belief that they had ushered in a democratic republic in which the dreams and aspirations of the mass of people would be achieved.

33. Women are under-represented in governance and decision making positions. At present, women occupy less than 8% of the Cabinet positions, less than 9% of seats in High Courts and the Supreme Court, and less than 12% of administrators and managers are women. In June 2009, out of 40 Cabinet Ministers, there were only three female Cabinet Ministers. There were only 4 female Ministers of State (MOS), out of 38 MOS in 2009. As on June 2009, there was no female judge out of 24 Judges in the Supreme Court. In the High Courts, there were only 51 female judges among the total of 649 judges.

34. However, through the vehicle of the Panchayati Raj Institutions and Urban Local Bodies more than one million

women have entered active political life in India, owing to one-third reservation in these bodies through the 73rd and 74th Amendments to the Constitution. These amendments have spearheaded an unprecedented social experiment, which is playing itself out in more than 500,000 villages that are home to more than 600 million people. Women are heading one-third of the panchayats and are gradually learning to use their new prerogatives, have transformed local governance by sensitizing the State to the issues of poverty, inequality and gender injustice. Since the creation of the quota system, local women–the vast majority of them being illiterate and poor – have come to occupy as much as 54% of the seats, spurring the election of increasing numbers of women at the district, provincial and national levels. Since the onset of PRI, the percentages of women in various levels of political activity have gone up to 36.7% in 2007.

35. According to National Family Health Survey –III in the rural sector currently married women take 26% decisions regarding obtaining health care for herself and 7.6% in case of purchasing major household items. 10% decisions are taken by females in respect of visiting their family or relatives. For urban areas, these figures are 29.7 %, 10.4 % and 12.2 % respectively.

36. In the age group of 15-19 years, 46% of women are not involved in any kind of decision making. In the rural sector, 23.4 % females are not involved in any decision-making while, in the urban sector, only 13.9 % of urban resident women are not involved in any decision making. It is found that 32.7% illiterate women, 21.6% unemployed women are not involved in any decision making. For the country as a whole, 59.6% have access to money.

Women and Men in India, 2012

A publication by the Central Statistics Office under the Ministry of Statistics and Programme Implementation, Government of India. The highlights:

Population and Vital Statistics

1. As per Census 2011, the population of India is 1210.19 million comprising 586.47 million (48.5%) females and 623.72 million (51.5%) males. Females have a share of 48.1% in the urban population and of 48.6% in the rural population.
2. The average annual exponential growth rate of population during 2001-2011 is 1.64%. The decadal growth rate during the same period stands at 17.64% which is 3.90% less than that during 1991-2011.
3. In the age-group 0-6 years, the share of female child population is 47.8% of the total child population in that age-group. Among the States, this share varies between 45.4% (Haryana) and 49.3% (Mizoram).
4. The sex-ratio (number of women per 1000 men) is 940 in 2011 which shows continued improvement over the sex ratios of 927 in 1991 and 933 in 2001. Among the States, in Census 2011, Kerala has the highest sex□ratio of 1084 and Haryana has the lowest of 877.
5. The mean age at effective marriage for females stands at 21.0 years in 2010. Among the major States, the highest mean age at effective marriage is 22.6 years for Kerala and the lowest is 20.1 years for Rajasthan.
6. Of the 48.7% never married persons in 2010, women had a share of 43.8% compared with 53.5% for men.
7. Total Fertility Rate (TFR) has come down from 3.2 in 1999 to 2.5 in 2010. The General Fertility Rate (GFR) during the same period has decreased from 103.2 to 83.9. The age-

specific fertility rate is highest (198.6) in the age-group 20-24 years followed by 156.8 in the age-group 20-24 years and 66.0 in the age-group 30-34 years.

8. Historically, the age-specific mortality rate is the lowest for both males and females in the age-group 10-14 years. The mortality rate among females across all ages is 6.7 and that among males is 7.7 for the year 2010.
9. Out of 150.18 million households in the rural areas in 2004-05, 16.67 million (11.1%) are Female Headed Households. In the urban sector, out of the total of 56.97 million households, 4.85 million (10.9%) are Female Headed.
10. Keeping with the past trend, the share of rural migrant females stood at a high level of 47.7% compared with a meager 5.4% of their male counterparts in 2007-08. The share of urban female migrants was 45.6% compared with 25.9% for males during the same period.
11. 60.8% of the rural migrant females migrated due to marriage followed by 29.4% due to movement of parents/earning member in 2007-08. A high 55.7% of the male migrants migrated due to employment reasons followed by 25.2% due to movement of parents/earning member in the same period.

Health and Well Being

12. The female Infant Mortality Rate (IMR) was 49 compared with the male IMR of 46 and the overall IMR of 47 in 2010. Among the major States, the highest overall IMR of 62 was observed in Madhya Pradesh and the lowest of 13 in Kerala in 2010.
13. Life Expectancy at Birth (LEB) has increased more among women compared to men. It is observed that in 2002-06 LEB for males was 62.6 years compared to 64.2 years for females.

14. 47.0% of the deliveries took place at a health facility in 2007-08. Share of women who received ante natal care was 76.9% during this period.
15. The Maternal Mortality Ratio has come down from 254 during 2004-06 to 212 during 2007-09.
16. 57.4% women in rural areas and 50.9% women in urban areas suffered from anemia during 2005-06. The share of anemic women across the age-groups 15-19 years, 20-29 years, 30-39 years and 40-49 years is centered around 55% during the same period. Among the States, prevalence of anemia was the highest in Assam and Jharkhand, both at 69.5%, and it was the lowest in Kerala at 32.8%.
17. The share of deliveries in hospitals, maternity/ nursing homes, health centers, etc. is 40.8% while the deliveries assisted by doctors, trained 'dais', trained midwives, trained nurses, etc. constitute another 48.8%.
18. Over 99% of married women know about any of the methods of contraception. The awareness about the female sterilization is very high in both urban and rural areas. The rural women are found to be less aware about the traditional methods of contraception (55.5%) compared with the urban women (62.4%).
19. During 2010-11, the share of unprotected couples was 59.6%. At 26.7%, sterilization was the most preferred method of family planning followed by IUD at 5.7%, oral pill at 4.1% and CC at 3.9%.
20. 2.2% women in India drink alcohol, 10.8% chew paan masala and 1.4% women smoke currently.

Participation in Economy

21. The workforce participation rate of females in rural sector was 26.1 in 2009-10 (NSS 64th Round) while that for males was 54.7. In Urban sector, it was 13.8 for females and 54.3 for males. Among the States/Union Territories,

workforce participation rate of females in the rural sector was the highest in Himachal Pradesh at 46.8% and in the urban sector it was the highest in Mizoram at 28.8%.

22. In the rural sector, 55.7% females were self-employed, 4.4% females had regular wage/salaried employment and 39.9% females were casual labourers compared with 53.5%, 8.5% and 38.0% males in the same categories respectively.
23. A total of 20.4% women were employed in the organized sector in 2010 with 17.9% working in the public sector and 24.5% in the private.
24. The labour force participation rate of women across all age-groups was 20.8 in rural sector and 12.8 in urban sector compared with 54.8 and 55.6 for men in the rural and urban sectors respectively in 2009-10 (NSS 64th Round).
25. The unemployment rate for women of all ages was 2.4 compared with 2.0 for men in the rural areas in 2009-10. It was 7.0 for women and 3.1 for men in urban areas during the same period. Among the States/Union Territories, the highest unemployment rate for women in rural sector was observed in Chandigarh (51.1%) and in the urban sector in Dadra and Nagar Haveli (60.0%) in 2009-10.
26. Of the total job seekers registered with employed exchanges, women constituted 32.5% in 2009.
27. The female share of total Central Government employment stood at 10.0% in 2009.
28. The share of female employees in the scheduled commercial banks was 15.9% in 2009 which rose slightly to 16.6% in 2010.
29. In 2009-10, the average wage/salary received by regular wage/salaried employees of age 15-59 years was Rs. 155.87 per day for females compared with Rs. 249.15 per day for males in rural areas. For urban areas, it was Rs. 308.79 and Rs. 377.16 per day for females and males respectively.

30. In 2010, the number of accounts operated by females in all commercial banks was 153.18 crores compared with 487.37 crore accounts operated by males. The deposit amount was Rs. 517209.74 crore for females and Rs. 1838826.25 crore for males.
31. In 2011-12, the share of women Swarojgaris (self-employed) in the total Swarojgaris assisted under the Swarnjayanti Gram Swarozgar Yojna (Golden Jubilee Rural Self Employment Scheme)) stood at 69.4%.
32. The share of women in the person days employed through MGNREGA stood at 48.3% in 2011-12 (all districts with rural areas).
33. According to the pilot Time Use Survey conducted in 18,620 households spread over six selected States, namely, Haryana, Madhya Pradesh, Gujarat, Orissa, Tamil Nadu and Meghalaya during the period June 1998 to July 1999, women spent about 2.1 hours per day on cooking food and about 1.1 hours on cleaning the households and utensils. Men's participation in these activities was nominal. Taking care of children was one of the major responsibilities of women, as they spent about 3.16 hours per week on these activities as compared to only 0.32 hours by males.

Literacy and Education

34. As per Census 2011, 74.0% of the population is literate comprising 65.5% females and2.1% males. The incremental increase over Census 2001 of 11.8% for females is higher than 6.8% for males.
35. Among the States/Union Territories, the female literacy rate is the highest in Kerala at 92.0% followed by Mizoram at 89.4%. The highest male literacy rate is observed in Lakshadweep at 96.1% followed by Kerala at 96.0% as per Census 2011.
36. As per NSS 64th Round, 2007-08, of the currently attending students aged 5-29 years, 69.2% females in primary schools,

65.6% females in the middle schools and 56.8% females in secondary and higher secondary schools were attending Government schools. The share of males is across the board lower at 65.4%, 64.0% and 55.6% in the respective categories.

37. Share of females getting free education/ exemption from tuition fee and receiving different types of incentives is higher than that for males in all the three levels of school education. However, the average annual expenditure for females is lower than that of males.

38. The main reasons of females never attending school are 'expensive cost of education', 'not interested in studies', 'education is not considered necessary' and 'required for household work'.

39. The Gross Enrolment Ratio (GER) for females at the primary level stood at 115.39 compared with 115.55 for males in 2009-10 indicating parity in GER. At the middle classes level, the GER for females was 78.30 while that for males was 84.53.

40. The Gross Attendance Ratio for females in the classes I-V in rural areas was 103 compared with 106 for males in 2007-08 (NSS 64th Round). The Net Attendance Ratio was observed to be 83 and 86 for females and males respectively in the rural areas in the classes I-V.

41. The Drop-out Rates were observed to be 27.25 and 30.25 for females and males respectively in the classes I-V in 2009-10. These were 44.39 and 40.59 in classes I-VIII and 51.97 and 53.38 in classes I-X for females and males respectively.

Participation in Decision Making

42. In 2012, women occupied only 8 out of 74 Ministerial positions in the Central Council of Ministers. There were 2 women judges out of 26 judges in the Supreme Court

and there were only 54 women judges out of 634 judges in different High Courts.

43. According to National Family Health Survey–III (2005-06) in the rural sector currently married women take 26% decisions regarding obtaining health care for herself and 7.6% in case of purchasing major household items. 10% decisions are taken by females in respect of visiting their family or relatives. For urban areas, these figures are 29.7 %, 10.4 % and 12.2 % respectively.

44. In the age group of 15-19 years, 46% of women are not involved in any kind of decision making. In the rural sector, 23.4 % females are not involved in any decision-making while, in the urban sector, only 13.9 % of urban resident women are not involved in any decision making. It is found that 32.7% illiterate women, 21.6% unemployed women are not involved in any decision making. For the country as a whole, 59.6% have access to money.

Crime against Women

45. Cruelty by husband and relatives continues to occupy the highest share (43.4%) among the crimes committed against women in 2011 followed by molestation (18.8%). 15.6% cases are that of kidnapping and abduction, 10.6% of rape, 3.8% of dowry deaths and 3.7% of sexual harassment.

46. 10.4% cases of cruelty by husband and relatives underwent trial by the Courts of Law in 2011 and conviction was done in 8.3% cases. The highest conviction rate of 16.5% was observed for the crime 'importation of girls' and the lowest of 4.0% for 'indecent representation of women'.

47. Out of a total 24270 victims, there were 875 victims who were less than 10 years of age, 1707 in the age-group 10-14 years, 4646 in the age-group 14-18 years, 13264 in the age-18-30 years, 3637 in the age-group of 30-50 years and 141 in the age-group greater than 50 years.

48. In 2011, of the total Juvenile Delinquency, 5.8% were girls. Also, the rate of incidence of the crime per lakh population was 2.1.

India in International Arena

49. India ranks 134 in 2011 among 187 countries in terms of the UNDP Human Development Index (HDI) and Gender Inequality Index (GII).

11
Crime against Women in India

Over 32000 murders, 19,000 rapes, 7500 dowry deaths and 36500 molestation cases are the violent crimes reported in India in 2006 against women. There are many instances of crime especially against women go unreported in India. These are figures released by the National Crime Records Bureau recently. While Madhya Pradesh is worst off among the states, the national capital New Delhi continues to hold on to its reputation of being the most unsafe city in India. Delhi takes the top slot for crimes ranging from murders and rapes to dowry deaths and abductions.

It reflects country's law and order situation when its capital is a cauldron of crime. Instead of leading the way in tackling crime, Delhi only seems to do worse year after year. For instance while the national crime rate declined negligibly by .02 % in 2006; Delhi's rate grew to 357.2more than double the national average of 167.7.

Rape is the fastest growing crime in the country today and as many as 18 women are assaulted in some form or the other every hour across India. Over the last few months cases of rapes and assault have made it to the headlines with alarming frequency. Mumbai watched with shame as an ugly mob attacked women on New Year's Eve. In Latur a 14 year old was raped and killed by four young men. In Konark four men were charged with dragging a woman out of a bus and gang raping her. It is an ordeal simply to file a police report and the investigations thereafter have been stories of apathy and downright humiliation meted out to the victims. Where convicted, punishments have ranged from capital punishments to a day in jail.

Equally horrific are news reports of foreign tourists being sexually assaulted. Recently an American was molested in Pushkar, a British journalist raped in Goa, Canadian girls attacked in Kumarakom to list the few instances. It looks like that India as a nation has ceased to know how to treat women as human beings who have a right to dignity and safety. The crime against tourists is against our culture of "atithi devo bhava' Government has decided to meet and discuss with the state government the safety of women tourists as a reaction from the fear that such incidents will impact India's image.

Despite the trauma women across all classes are reporting crimes such as rape and assault and do not feel helpless or abandoned by family or society as was the prevalent case before. Society is changing and government is forced to take action as it has run out of excuses such as society's mindset or class divide.

37. Crimes against women have become universal reality for all societies. Among the crimes committed against women in 2008, torture shares the highest percentage (42%), followed by molestation (21%). 11.0% cases are that of rape, 11.7% of kidnapping and abduction, and 1.0% of immoral trafficking. It is also significant to note that 6.0% cases are of sexual harassment and 4.1% of dowry deaths.
38. Out of a total 20771 victims, there were 617 victims who were less than 10 years of age, 1355 in the age group 10-14 years, 3152 in the age group 14-18 years, 11984 in the age group 18-23 years, 3530 in the age group of 30-50 years and 133 in the age group greater than 50 years.
39. In 2008, of the total juvenile delinquency, 5.0% were girls. Also, the rate of incidence of the crime per lakh population was 2.1.

India in International Arena

40. India ranks 134 in 2009 among 178 countries in terms of the UNDP Human Development Index (HDI) and 114 in terms of Gender Development Index (GDI).

Crime against Women in India-II

"A society that is unable to respect, protect and nurture its women and children loses its moral moorings and runs adrift."
S. Chatterjee

Introduction:

Centuries have come, and centuries have gone, but the plight of women is not likely to change. Time has helplessly watched women suffering in the form of discrimination, oppression, exploitation, degradation, aggression, humiliation. In Indian society, woman occupies a vital position and venerable place. The Vedas glorified women as the mother, the creator, one who gives life and worshipped her as a 'Devi' or Goddess. But their glorification was rather mythical for at the same time, in India women found her totally suppressed and subjugated in a patriarchal society. Indian women through the countries remained subjugated and oppressed because society believed in clinging on to orthodox beliefs for the brunt of violence—domestic as well as public, Physical, emotional and mental. Male violence against women is worldwide phenomenon. Fear of violence is an important factor in the lives of most women. Fear of violence is the cause of lack of participation in every sphere of life. There are various forms of crime against women. Sometimes it is even before birth, some times in the adulthood and other phrases of life. In the Indian society, position of women is always perceived in relation to the man. This perception has given birth to various customs and practices. Violence against women both inside and outside of their home has been a crucial issue in the contemporary Indian society. Women in India constitute near about half of its population and most of them are grinding under the socio-cultural and religious structures. One gender has been controlling the space of the India's social economic, political and religious fabric since time immemorial. The present study felt the need that in the era of globalization and modernization the present trends of crimes against women is on increase. Recently the brutal gang rape against 23 year student in Delhi again sparked the debate on Indian mental set up and existing law and order in the Country.

Various legislations for safeguarding the women

There are various legislation has been incorporated regarding the safeguarding of the women: Various Legislation for safeguarding crime against women, classified under two categories:

The Crime under Indian Penal Code (IPC):

- Rape (Section 376 IPC)
- Kidnapping and abduction for specified purpose (Section 363-373 IPC)
- Homicide for dowry, Dowry death or their attempts. (Sec. 302/304-B IPC)
- Torture both mental and physical (Sec.498-A –IPC)
- Sexual Harassment (Sec. 509 IPC)
- Importation of girls (Up to 21 years of age) (Sec. 366-B IPC)

1. The Crimes under the Special and local Laws (SLL) - Gender specific laws

- Immoral Traffic (Prevention) Act, 1956.
- Dowry Prohibition Act, 1961
- Indecent Representation of Women (Prohibition) Act, 1986.
- Commission of Sati (Prevention) Act, 1987.

Another danger in India is that, Indian law does not differentiate between major and minor rape. Rape in India has been described by Radha Kumar as one of the "India's most common crime against women." 1 Rape cultures are nourished by norms, attitudes, and practices that trivialize, tolerate, or even condone violence against women. They are further normalized if there is impunity for perpetrators either due to a lack of effective legal mechanisms or apathy to prosecuting crimes against women. The need for a new law on sexual assault was felt as the present law does not define and reflect the various kinds of sexual assault that women are subjected to in our country. The Supreme Court in Sakshi vs. union of India had recognized the inadequacies in the law relating to rape and had suggested that the legislature should bring about the required changes.

Crime head	2001	2006	2007	2008	2009	2010
Rape (Section 376 IPC)	16075 (1.6%)	19348 (1.7%)	20737 (1.8%)	21467 (1.9%)	21397 (1.8%)	22172 (1.9%)

"In 2010 there were 22,193 victims of Rape out of 22,172 reported cases in the country. 8.9% (1,975) of the total victims of Rape were girls under 14 years of age, while 16.1% (3,570) were teenage girls (14-18 years). 57.4% (12,749) were women in the age-group 18-30 years. 3,763 victims (17.0%) were in the age-group of 30-50 years while 0.6% (136) was over 50 years of age."

Crime against women Percentage Distribution during 2010

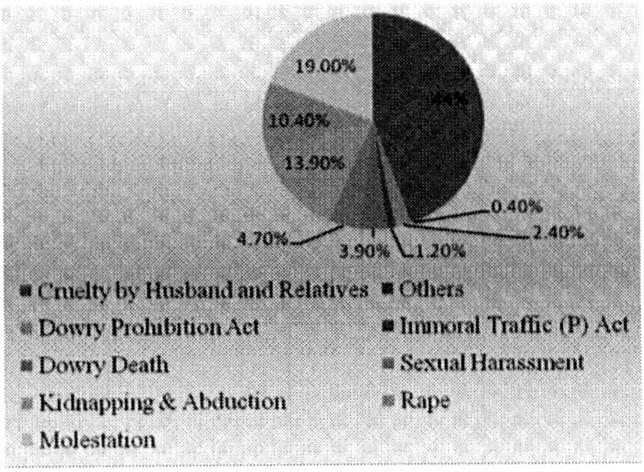

Proportion of Crime against women (IPC) towards total IPC crimes

S.No.	Year	Total IPC crime	Crime against women (IPC cases)	% to total IPC cases.
1.	2006	18,78,293	1,54,158	8.2
2.	2007	19,89,673	1,74,921	8.8
3.	2008	20,93,379	1,86,617	8.9
3.	2009	21,21,345	2,03,804	9.2
4.	2010	22,24,831	2,13,585	9.6

As per the above data crime rate trend analysis against women in India shows clearly the sharp increased crime rate from (8.2%) in 2006 to (9.6 %) in 2010 in the last five years. which is a serious matter from the safety and security point of Indian women.

Crime against women in India is increasing daily. Here are some glaring facts about crime against women in India from the latest National Crime report 2011.

West Bengal reported 12.7% of total such cases in the country (29,133 out of 2, 28,650). Tripura reported the highest crime rate (37.0) as compared to the National average rate of 18.9.

The proportion of IPC crimes committed against women towards total IPC crimes has increased during last 5 years from 8.8% in the year 2007 to 9.4% during the year 2011.

Madhya Pradesh has reported the highest number of Rape cases (3,406), Molestation (6,665) and Importation of Girls (45) accounting for 14.1%, 15.5% and 56.3% respectively of total such cases reported in the country.

Andhra Pradesh has reported 42.7% (3,658) of Sexual Harassment cases.

The Cases under Immoral Traffic (Prevention) Act decreased by 2.6% (from 2,499 in 2010 to 2,435 in 2011), Andhra

Pradesh (497) followed by Tamil Nadu (420) reported the highest incidence of 24.1% and 17.2% respectively of total cases (2,435) under Immoral Traffic (Prevention) Act.

Highest cases of Kidnapping & Abduction 21.2% (7,525) and Dowry Deaths 26.9% (2,322) were reported in Uttar Pradesh. Offenders were known to the victims in 92.9% of Rape cases (22,549 out of 24,270).

A total of 33,789 cases of crime against women were reported from 53 mega cities out of 2, 28,650 cases reported in the country during 2011. And rate of crime in these cities at 21.0 was comparatively higher as compared to national rate at 18.9.

Among 53 cities, Delhi (City) accounted for 13.3% (4,489) of total such crimes followed by Bengaluru 5.6% (1,890) and Hyderabad 5.5% (1,860).

Crimes against women in Cities:

Crimes rates are much higher in big cities than in either small cities or rural areas. "There is a litany of theory about the connection between cities and crime. Indeed some of the most important of the ideas on crime and cities has been discussed at early stages of modern Sociology by Emile Durkheim, George Simmel and Max weber. Wirth (1938) claimed that urban crime reflects the more anonymous and unstable nature of urban life. Jacob (1961) focuses on the emptiness of urban streets, and argues that cities only abet crimes when urban neighborhood loses their traditional social structure." A study conducted by NAVTEQ in 2011 regarding safety of women in Delhi reveals that, 51 percentages of the women surveyed in Delhi, Kolkata, and Chennai felt unsafe while travelling on roads while 73 % said that they were scared of travelling at night. TNS Market Research claims 87 per cent women regarded Delhi as most unsafe city while Mumbai was touted as the safest city by 74 per cent women.

There are some of the bright ideas have been given but they are still remaining in the papers:

Date	Ideas
25th April 2008	Reception hostel to be set up in each district as transit accommodation for women in distress.
5th Feb. 2009	Women Constable to be deployed in slums and areas near lacking civic amenities. They should interact with women and identify habitual /potential harassers /molesters to take preventive action.
28th May 2009	Action to be taken against stalkers of women like making them signs a bond pledging good behavior.
11th June 2009	Patrolling by women constable /officers in slum and other congested areas should be intensified.
22nd Oct 2009	Delhi Police commissioner should write to transport commissioner advising that antecedents of all drivers of public service vehicles must be verified by police. Drivers should also carry biometric photo ID.
22nd Dec.2010	Constable should be posted at bus stops to instill a sense of security in women commuters.
28th Oct 2011	All DTC bus stops in DU's North and South Campuses should be covered by police.

12
Women's Work: Has Anything Changed?

One striking feature of the latest National Sample Survey round results is the apparent decline in female employment in 2009-10 compared with 2004-05. This edition of Macro Scan examines this feature in more detail to isolate the important processes and factors at work.

There has already been much discussion about the low rates of employment growth in India that are reflected in the latest large sample round to the NSSO surveys.

One of the features that have contributed to this decline in employment growth in the most recent five-year period is the slump in female employment, which can be considered as one of the more important elements in the overall deceleration of employment generation.

As was shown in a previous edition of Macro Scan, applying the participation rates of the NSSO survey of 2009-10 to interpolated population figures from Censuses 2001 and 2011 shows that total female employment actually declined at an annual rate of 1.72 per cent between 2004-05 and 2009-10, while male employment (mostly in casual work) showed a slight increase, albeit much lower than in the previous period, at the rate of 1.72 per cent.

Disturbing Trend

Clearly, this is a significant and potentially very disturbing result, especially given that women's work participation rates are already quite low in India compared to most other parts of the developing world.

It should be borne in mind, of course, that work participation rates as described by official surveys are not really good indicators of the productive contributions of women.

This is particularly so in large parts of India, where much of the economic activity of women, whether in the home or outside, is simply not recognised as such by other household members and even by the women themselves.

A significant part of women's work is not just unpaid, therefore: it is also socially unrecognized. This is true of not just social reproduction, but other economic activity where women's work is rendered invisible by social perceptions.

That is why many social scientists take women's work participation rate as one of the proxy indicators of women's overall status in society and of gender empowerment.

It is not just because paid work provides income individually to women rather than to male members of the household. It is also because the productive contribution of women is typically less recognised in societies where women are undervalued in general.

Interesting Features

Chart 1 indicates the movement of female work participation rates in India from the late 1970s. Several features of interest emerge from this chart. First, rural participation rates are nearly three times the urban rates, though they still remain relatively low at only around 30 per cent compared to around double that in most East Asian countries.

Second, the longer term trend appears one of gentle decline even within these relatively low rates, which is truly remarkable in a rapidly growing economy. The experience of most other developing countries in phases of rapid growth has been that of rapid and often substantial increase in female overt work participation, as dynamic capitalism tends to draw in women to expand domestic labour supply for paid employment.

The third feature that seems to come out from Chart 1 is that if anything, 2004-05 is a bit of an outlier in terms of increasing female work participation, whereas 2009-10 indicates a reversion to the longer term trend of gradual decline. If this is indeed true (which of course requires further examination) then it suggests that inadequate capture of women's work in the latest sample round may not be the most important reason for the evident decline. Rather, the more pressing question should be why women's work participation rates have been so low in India and have remained low despite rapid economic growth and many other changes in society.

Real Paradox

Suppose we even consider that for whatever reason, 2004-05 was an unusual year within this dataset. So let us consider the change in women's employment status for the decade as a whole, that is, from 1999-2000 to 2009-10. Table 1 provides the details for women in the age group of 15 years and above, and even these are quite startling.

Remember that the 2000s were a decade of unprecedented rapid GDP growth for the Indian economy. In this decade, the number of women aged 15 years or more increased by 86.5 million.

But only 8.9 per cent of them joined the labour force, and only 7.5 per cent of them were described as gainfully employed. This relative lack of increase in the number of working women in a period of major economic expansion is not just unusual; it is also hard to explain in terms of most standard economic approaches.

More in Education

The really large increase – accounting for more than 20 per cent of the increase in number of women overall – was in education. Of course this was dominantly confined to younger women, but it is clearly a process to be greatly welcomed. Chart 2 shows that the most recent period has experienced the biggest increase in the number of young women in education. This is particularly prevalent for urban girls aged 15-19 years, nearly 70 per cent of whom are now studying as their principal activity. But the recent relatively fast increase in education for girls even in rural areas is a good sign.

When we look at the patterns of employment of the relatively few women who are recognised as gainfully employed, even in this aspect the apparent lack of change appears to be more striking than any dynamism. Chart 3 shows the distribution of women workers by type of contract. Once again, the year 2004-05 appears as an outlier, when there was apparently a big increase in self-employment and an associated decline in the share of casual work.

Obviously, we will need more disaggregated data to delve into the actual processes at work in this case, but a quick assessment suggests that in rural areas the medium term process has been of decline in self-employment and increase in casual work of women, with regular employment persistently occupying a negligible space.

Real Urban Story

In urban areas, as shown in Chart 4, a somewhat similar process seems to have been at work in terms of the relative shares of self-employed and casual workers. But the real story for urban women is the increase in regular employment, which has continued into the most recent years. When this was first observed for 2004-05, it created much joy in official circles, until it was pointed out the largest increase in urban regular employment of women was in the form of domestic service – as maids, cooks and cleaners, hardly the most desirable or dynamic forms of work. This accounted for 3 million more urban women workers in the period 1999-2000 to 2004-05, far exceeding the increase in "export-oriented" sectors such as garments, leather and IT-enabled activities.

We do not yet have the detailed data that will allow us to examine whether a similar process was at work in the most recent quinquennium. But in any case, that experience should give us pause in interpreting the current evidence, and not give rise to undue or premature celebration.

High Unemployment

The evidence on female unemployment rates adds to the uneasiness involved in including 2004-05, which seems more and more to have been an unusual year. Even excluding that year, Chart 5 suggests that open unemployment rates for women have remained at fairly high levels over the period of high economic growth. Throughout this period, more than 7 per cent of urban women who count themselves as in the labour force were unemployed and actively looking for work but not finding it, as their usual principal activity. In terms of current daily status – the activity that they pursued on an average day in the previous week – the rate of open unemployment has been even higher, at around 10 per cent. In rural areas, as expected, both rates were lower but still current daily status unemployment was significantly high at more than 8 per cent, and show a major increase compared to the late 1980s.

The other depressing feature that emerges from the latest round of NSS data is that economic growth has still not generated a process of employment diversification for women. Even more than men, and substantially so, women workers remain stuck in low value-added but arduous work in agriculture. Around two-thirds of women workers are still employed in agriculture as their principal economic activity, while the share for men workers has fallen to less than half.

Job Diversification

For the men and women, this is actually an appalling rate of employment diversification. Every single development success that we have seen in history has been associated with a movement of workers away from primary activities to more value-added work in secondary and tertiary sectors.

The stubborn domination of agriculture as the primary source of work for most of our workers (especially women) is a particular problem given the agrarian crisis that has persisted for nearly two decades in the countryside, which makes involvement in such work increasingly fraught and financially unviable. All in all, these patterns of women's work – and indeed therefore of men's work – amount to a severe indictment of the Indian growth story, in terms of what it is delivering to the bulk of Indian workers.

Women Employment

You can tell the condition of a nation by looking at the status of its women. **- Jawahar lal**

Women workforce constitutes an integral part of total workforce in India. On 31st March 2004, women constituted 19 per cent of the total workforce. The participation of women in the labour force has always been lower than that of men, in the rural as well as urban areas. The work participation rate for women has increased significantly. In 1981, work participation rate for women was only 19.67 per cent which increased up to 22.73 per cent in 1991 and 26.68 per cent in 2001. In the women workforce, women from rural areas are greater in number as compared to the urban women. Amongst rural women workers, a majority is employed in agriculture and some are employed in cottage industries. In the urban areas, women workers are primarily employed in the unorganized sectors. As on the 31st March, 2005 a total number of 50.16 lac women employees were engaged in the organized sector, out of which 26.21 lac (52.76 per cent) in the public sector and 20.95 lac (41.50 per cent) in the Private Sector and remaining 5.74% in unorganized sector.

Employment of women in public sector increased by 1.1 percent and by 2.5 percent in the private sector during 2004-2005. The zone wise analysis showed an increase of 8 percent in North-Eastern Zone, followed by Western Zone (5.3 per cent), Eastern Zone (3 per cent) and Central Zone (1.3per cent) and Northern Zone (1.2per cent). Only Southern Zone registered a marginal dip of 0.8 percent.

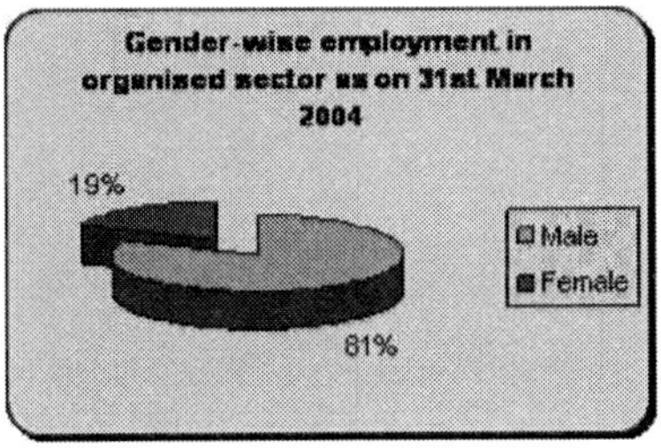

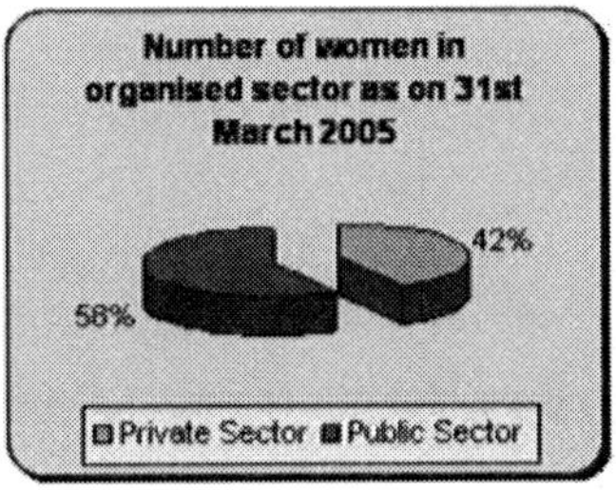

Some Vital Statistics

- The number of women job seekers has increased from 99.3 lakhs in 1999 to 106.1 lakhs in 2004. Thus the percentage of women job seekers to the total job-seekers has also increased from 24.6per cent in 1999 to 26.2per cent in 2004.

Table 1: Number of Women Job Seekers

Year	Number of Women (in lac)	Percentage to total
1999	99.3	24.6
2000	104.5	25.3

2001	108.8	25.9
2002	106	25.9
2003	107.5	26.0
2004	106.1	26.0

- Number of Educated Women Job Seekers as on December 2004 was 7537.7 thousand. Educated Women at the end of 2004 accounted for 25.8per cent of the total educated job-seekers.

Table 1: Number of Educated Women Job Seekers		
Year	**Number of Women (in lac)**	**Percentage to total**
2000	7911.7	27.1
2001	8525.6	28.1
2002	7921.4	26.8
2003	8032.4	26.6
2004	7537.7	25.8

- The state wise analysis reflects that Kerala has the maximum (21.1 lac) women job-seekers followed by West Bengal (19.3 lac) and Tamil Nadu (15.3 lac) while minimum number of women job-seekers are in Rajasthan (1.0 lac).
- The percentage of educated women job seekers among the total women job seekers has gone down from 73.3per cent to 70.4per cent in 2004.
- The work participation rate for women was 25.68 per cent in 2001. This shows an improvement over 22.73 per cent in 1991 and 19.67 per cent in 1981.
- Women workers constituted 19 per cent of the total organized sector employment in the country, as compared to 18.4 per cent in the previous year. As on 31st March, 2004, there were about 49.34 lacs women workers employed in the organized sector (Public and Private Sector).
- As far as industries are concerned, in 2005, the manufacturing industry faced a dip of 1.1per cent in women employment.

On the other hand, other industries reflected an increase in women employment. An increase of 7.8 per cent was registered in Wholesale and Retail Trade followed by 5.6 per cent in Mining and Quarrying, 5.5 per cent in Agriculture, Hunting, Forestry & Fishing, 5.2 per cent in Financing, Insurance Real Estate & Business Services, 1.7 per cent in Electricity, Gas & Water, 1.5 per cent in Construction, 1.4 per cent in Community, Social and Personal Services and 1.2 per cent in Transport, Storage & Communications.

Women Entrepreneur... New Face of Women

Women constitute almost half of the total population of world. Similarly in India also women constitute fifty percent of the total population.

Till the turn of the century, man has enjoyed a dominant position. But change in position technological innovation and modern way of thinking can reduce the disparity between man and women, and bring about equality and equity between them, the need of the hour in women empowerment both through provision of employment and enterprise creation. Typologically, the former leader to endogenous empowerment and the latter give rise to exogenous empowerment.

Women entreprenurer's have been making a significant impact in all segments of the economy in Canada, Great Britain, Germany Australia and US.

The areas choosen by women are retail trade, restaurants, hotels, education, cultural, cleaning insurance and manufacturing.

It is the group of women or single women running an enterprise or company in order to earn profit. Now days because of women empowerment women are stepping-stone into the industries and are taking the place of men. Now a day's women's are running several business like beauty parlours, switching shops, boutiques, etc.

Women entrepreneurs may be defined as a woman or a group of women who initiate, organize and run a business enterprise. In terms of Schunpeterian concept of innovative entrepreneurs, women who innovate, initiate or adopt a business activity are called business entrepreneur.

The Government of India has defined women entrepreneurs based on women participation in equity and employment of a business enterprise. Accordingly, a woman entrepreneur is defined as an enterprise owned and controlled by a woman having a minimum financial interest of 51% of the capital and giving at least 51% of the employment generated in the enterprise to a woman.

They have made their marks in business because of the following reasons:

They want to improve their mettle in innovation and competitive jobs.

They want the change to control the balance between their families and responsibility and their business levels.

They want new challenges and opportunities for self fulfillment.

Role of women as an Entrepreneur's:

1) Imaginative: It refers to the imaginative approach or original ideas with competitive market. Well-planned approach is needed to examine the existing situation and to identify the entrepreneurial opportunities. It further implies that women entrepreneurs have association with knowledgeable people and contracting the right organization offering support and services.
2) Attribute to work hard: Enterprising women have further ability to work hard. The imaginative ideas have to come to a fair play. Hard work is needed to build up an enterprise..

3) Persistence: Women entrepreneurs must have an intention to fulfill their dreams. They have to make a dream transferred into an idea enterprise; Studies show that successful women work hard.
4) Ability and desire to take risk the desire refers to the willingness to take risk and ability to the proficiency in planning making forecast estimates and calculations.
5) Profit earning capacity: she should have a capacity to get maximum return out of invested capital.

A Woman entrepreneur has also to perform all the functions involved in establishing an enterprise. These include idea generation, and screening, determination of objectives, project preparation, product analysis, determination of forms of business organization, completion of formal activities, raising funds, procuring men machine materials and operations of business.

Fredrick Harbiscon, has enumerated the following five functions of a women entrepreneur's :

Exploration of the prospects of starting a new business enterprise.

Undertaking a risk and handling of economic uncertainties involved in business.

Introduction of innovations, imitations of innovations.

Co ordination, administration and control.

Supervision and leadership.

In nutshell, women entrepreneur are those women who think of a business enterprise, initiate it organize and combine the factors of production, operate the enterprise, undertake risk and handle economic uncertainties involved in running a business enterprise.

What Is the Role of Women in Indian Politics? Growing Stronger...

India should work towards empowering women economically -- through microfinance programs -- and also encourage greater participation of women leaders in panchayats, or village councils, writes author Shoba Narayan in this opinion piece.

The ink-stained polls of the world's largest democracy have delivered their verdict and India waits with bated breath to learn whether Prime Minister Manmohan Singh's second administration will be different than the first. While India exults after yet another peacefully concluded election, one question remains: What is the role of women in Indian politics? The answer is both big and small. Typical of India, it contains contradictions.

On the one hand, India falls in the lowest quartile with respect to the number of women in parliament (9.1%). Even the UAE, with 22.5%, has more women representatives, according to the UN's 2008 survey of women in politics. That said, the recently concluded 15th Lok Sabha elections have delivered a record 59 women as members of Parliament, the highest since independence, raising their parliamentary participation to 10.9%. Seventeen of these women are under 40. And representation of women leaders at the grassroots level in India is nearly 50%, especially since the passing of the 73rd amendment in 1992, which allotted one-third of all seats to women. The Panchayati raj, that bedrock of rural government, has fostered more and more women participants and leaders. Some states, like Karnataka, had inducted women into rural politics even before it was mandated by the constitution. Several states, including Madhya Pradesh, Himachal Pradesh, Bihar and most recently, Uttarkhand, have allotted not just the required 33% of panchayat seats for women but increased it to 50%.

Beating the Odds

The rise of Indian women as panchayat leaders is a spectacular achievement given that India has one of the worst records with respect to the way it treats the female sex. Malnourished, suppressed, uneducated, violated and discriminated against, Indian women have the odds stacked against them. Even birth is a hurdle, thanks to widespread female infanticide in rural areas. But for every Saroja who will be married at 13 because her mother, a devadasi (prostitute) in Chikanahalli Village, Karnataka, cannot afford to pay a dowry, there is a Lakshmi, who is serving her second-term as the panchayat leader of Kadinamala village in Kotagiri district. There is a Kenchamma of Nereleke grampanchayat in rural Karnataka, who survived life threats during her two terms as council leader. An illiterate Dalit, Kenchamma could not read or write. Perhaps as a result of her personal travails, she made sure that she brought education to all the children in her village, including a disabled child.

Talking to these women is a lesson in humility. Instead of the outrage and anger that urban feminist's project, these women panchayat leaders speak with clear-minded realism about opportunities and costs. For many women who are attending a panchayat meeting means they are sacrificing a day's wage. It means assuming leadership for the first time in their lives and then subsuming it at home to serve in-laws and husband. For

Kenchamma, it meant leaving her one-year-old son to other caregivers while she learned the ropes of politics.

Ask these women about political reform, and their answers reflect concerns that every women and mother can relate to. They focus on three things: healthcare, education, and the funds to make these two things happen. Kenchamma, a trained midwife, established health camps to improve awareness among the villagers. She also knew from personal experience that, often, it is the mothers who neglect their health the most. Simplistic as it seems, solving health and education is a common thread among panchayat leaders, whether they are men or women. The third concern is figuring out how to save or raise enough money to accomplish their goals.

Most villagers -- in India and across the world -- either don't go to banks or don't have access to them. Instead, they borrow from each other, buy jewelry and save in what Melinda Gates calls, "risky and inefficient ways" in a recent piece she wrote in Newsweek. For most of these villagers, a child's illness is even something as treatable as malaria, can wipe out several months of savings, sending a family into spiraling deeper into debt. The answer, according to the Gates Foundation -- no slouch when it comes to solving global problems in an accountable manner -- is "bringing safe financial service to the doorsteps of the poor." As a means to that end, the Foundation has pledged $350 million for microfinance, whose beneficiary is primarily women.

Microfinance and Economic Empowerment

Geeta, 32, would be a typical candidate. An orphan at age three, Geeta was raised by her elder sister. She didn't go to school and was married to an alcoholic uncle when she was a teenager. Today, she works as a housemaid in Bangalore to feed her family of four: Her husband, her two sons and herself. Geeta's life goal is to educate her two sons. But she lives in a cycle of debt --

borrowing to repay past loans, to make annual school payments for her sons, to cover family events like weddings and every time someone in the family falls sick. Geeta, it so happens, works in my house.

Two years ago, Geeta heard about Janalakshmi, a microfinance company, from some women in her neighborhood. She joined a group of women and borrowed Rs. 30,000 with the understanding that they would help each other not default on interest payments and take turns reaping the benefits of the loan. Each group has a leader who guarantees the interest payment to the microfinance institution and in turn, the leader invites women she trusts into the group so that they can borrow larger amounts. For now, Geeta's microfinance loan is only allowing her to pay back her previous debts, but she dreams of the day when she can borrow enough money for a down payment on a home.

More and more entities are recognizing the power of micro-loans and how they can elevate an entire segment of society. And the route to the underserved is frequently through women, thanks to models based on Grameen Bank and others. Chennai-based Equitas, for instance, only works with women. In March, the Indus Entrepreneurs (TiE) launched Stree Shakti, a platform for training women entrepreneurs at all levels of Indian society. Goldman Sachs's ambitious "10,000 Women" program aims to train and develop women entrepreneurs across the globe by pairing them with resources in the West. In all these cases, women serve as the lynchpin for programs; whether they are rural Self Help Groups (SHG) or global programs that aspire to foster entrepreneurship.

Microfinance is not the only answer to solving the poor's problems but it is one good way to help women help themselves. Women self-help groups are burgeoning all across India, and study after study shows that they successfully impact women and bring them out of poverty. In an article that appeared in the

December 2007 issue of UNDP's Poverty in Focus, researchers Ranjula Bali Swain and Fan Yang Wallington of Uppsala University in Sweden examine the link between microfinance and women's empowerment using household sample data collected from five states in India in 2000 and 2003. Their results "strongly demonstrate" that there is a clear link between women's participation in a Self Help Group (SHG) and their empowerment.

The good news, at least in India, is that these microfinance initiatives are reaching bigger swathes of the underserved. The Indian School of Microfinance for Women (ISMW), for instance, goes one step deeper into the problem. Based in Ahmadabad and chaired by social activist and SEWA founder Ela Bhatt, the school recognizes that borrowing money is only one part of the triangle. Among other things, the school teaches women how to deal with the money they borrow through capacity building workshops, networking and providing knowledge resources. Simply put, it takes Goldman Sachs's global vision for women entrepreneurs and translates it into a deeper regional focus. The school's website lists 'hand-holding' as one of its goals. Participants of micro-credit schemes are taught financial planning and investing techniques that they can use on the ground and in their business.

While microfinance works to eradicate poverty, the next generation of Indian leaders, including Rahul Gandhi, has made social sectors its calling card. The rural development portfolio, which traditionally was one of the less-prized posts, has now vaulted to the top of the pecking order, thanks in large part to the Gandhi family which has aligned itself with the aam admi (poor people) in both its campaigning and future promises. When Manmohan Singh was asked in a recent television interview if he had any regrets about areas that he couldn't concentrate on in his first term that he would focus on in his second term, he said, "I'd like to work on agriculture, education and rural health."

Reforming Education

Panchayat women leaders have been especially active in bringing education to their villages even though they are frequently held hostage by caste politics and quotas. Rural education is a quagmire of poor policies that nobody in government seems to have the will to change. The recent Administrative Reforms Commission repeats a long-standing recommendation that the selection of school teachers in rural schools be delegated to each panchayat instead of making it state-wide and therefore subject to caste-based selection. Deploying state-selected teachers to rural schools in areas where they have no caste-based affiliation makes it a losing proposition from the get-go, according to some experts. Detractors contend that delegating teacher-selection to each panchayat will make it subject to bribes and corruption. But as one official in the Administrative Reforms Commission put it, small-scale rural corruption is better than the large-scale corruption

Panchayat leaders who don't have a say in the kind of teachers their village-schools attract end up focusing on infrastructure and other issues within their purview. Women panchayat leaders talk about building separate bathrooms for girls, which studies have shown will reduce the number of female drop-outs after puberty. They bring safe drinking water to their students. All these are not just palliatives, but are necessary developments in rural education.

It is easy to be cynical about yet another federal election that promises improvements to local government and to the lot of women. This time may be different, not just because of the number of women in parliament and the panchayats, but also because Rahul Gandhi, a rising star in Congress politics, is tapped to oversee the rural government portfolio. One can only hope that the Gandhi scion will free the portfolio of its state-level stranglehold and pass along more power to the people.

Non-partisan economists have long called for decentralized local governance as the only way to speed up the impact of reforms. To that, I would add two other objectives: wider access to micro-loans as an enabler, and genuinely empowering women in local governments to succeed.

13

Entrepreneurship Development for Competitive Small and Medium Enterprises

Entrepreneur Development for Competitive SMEs

Development for Competitive Small and Medium Enterprises

Small and Medium Enterprises or SMEs feature prominently in the countries.

They constitute the largest economic and business entities and assume a major role in employment generation. As such, many member countries place great importance on the development of the competitiveness of SMEs so that they can serve as the engine of growth for national economies.

A high level of competitiveness is attributable to a number of factors. These include appropriate business models and strategies, the ability to penetrate a market, and strong leadership.

The SMEs, being small enterprises will have to take into account other additional factors, such as access to capital and technological development. Many of the initiatives to develop competitiveness of the SMEs focus on the areas of financial and capital assistance, business matching and partnership with large corporations, and technological development.

Here, one is able to examine SME competitiveness through entrepreneurship development. Entrepreneurship is regarded as a type of business acumen which may be enhanced through improvements in know-how, skills, and competency. The specific focus on development of entrepreneurship is prompted by an underlying assumption that development of this skill will be a longer-lasting benefit than other forms of assistance such as technology, finance, and partnership arrangements.

The present theories prepared by a team of SME experts, policy-makers, and practitioners from the member countries of Bangladesh, India, Indonesia, Malaysia, Nepal, Pakistan, the Philippines, and Vietnam. It would like to express deep appreciations to all the contributors and the member countries participating in the discussion as well as to all other parties who have agreed to open their doors and provide access to the information and data that are necessary for the completion of this job. It is hoped that these discussions and experiences with the development of entrepreneurship in the SMEs in the selected member countries will provide practical ideas and concrete examples for the further development and competitiveness of SMEs in the Asia-Pacific region.

Entrepreneurship Development for Competitive Small and Medium Enterprises

In the new millennium, liberalization of trade borders has accelerated the flow of goods and

Services in the global markets; technological advancement and scientific development have had a multiplier effect on the opportunities and choices available to consumers, thus increasing competition and putting pressure on the performance of the individual firms and businesses within economies. Undoubtedly, this has led to the need to enhance productivity at the firm level, which is the driving force behind rate of return on investment—and which, in turn, determines the aggregate growth rates of an economy. These challenges have sequentially spurred governments to focus on factors influencing national competitiveness.

National competitiveness is based on numerous and diverse factors. There is a great deal of empirical evidence stressing the importance of a sound macroeconomic environment for growth.

However, macroeconomic stability alone is not sufficient to increase productivity. Economists today believe that factors like the institutional environment within which economic actors operate, the protection of property rights, the quality of the judicial system, corruption within the system, and the political processes are equally important. Further, factors influencing productivity levels, such as education and training, have emerged as key drivers of competitiveness. Yet these factors work influence different economies in different ways, primarily due to the stage of economic development, and these factors also evolve over time, given the rapid pace of technological development affecting productivity growth. Hence, in the year 2006, the criteria for the Global Competitiveness Index (GCI) were revised to include critical factors that drive productivity and competitiveness: institutions, infrastructure, macro economy, health and primary education, higher education and training, market efficiency, technological readiness, business sophistication, and innovation.

Competitiveness finds its ultimate expression in the prosperity that countries can sustain over time. Prosperity is sustainable if it is based on the level of productivity that companies can reach given the conditions they face in an economy. While competitiveness remains focused on macro economic, political, legal, and social circumstances that strengthen a successful economy, progress in these areas is necessary but not sufficient. Hence, the Business Competitiveness Index (BCI) has been developed, which ranks countries by their microeconomic competitiveness, identifies competitive strengths and weaknesses in terms of countries' business environment conditions and company operations and strategies, and provides an assessment of the sustainability of countries' current levels of prosperity.

The private sector can contribute to economic growth, job creation, and national income— and hence to national prosperity and competitiveness. Invariably, domestic private sector resources in any economy are much larger than actual or potential external resources. The private sector contributes substantially to the Gross Domestic Product (GDP), and thus unleashing domestic resources—both financial and entrepreneurial—is likely to create a more stable and sustainable pattern of growth. Governments are becoming more sensitive to the need to create a friendly business climate, supportive of the needs of the private sector.

Small and medium enterprises (SMEs), the major component of the private sector, can be engines of economic growth, cornerstones for creativity and innovation, and seedbeds of entrepreneurship. But in many countries SMEs operate in the informal sector, technologically backward, with low levels of human resource skills, weak management systems and entrepreneurial capabilities, unavailability of appropriate and timely information, insufficient use of information technology, poor product quality and standardization, and unfriendly environmental production processes—all of which contribute to widespread low productivity. These SME slack accesses to financing and long-term capital, the bases on which companies are built.

More than 90% of enterprises in the member countries are SMEs. They account for about 75% of the Gross Domestic Product, compared to 50% in the rest of the world. They play an important role in economic and social life, and they generate a large number of non-agricultural jobs, exports, sales, and value-added. Yet in most of these countries, SMEs face similar constraints and hence are low-productivity enterprises. Their contribution to national prosperity and competitiveness is evident from the rankings documented in the Global Competitiveness Report 2006–07.

GCI and BCI Ranks of Selected Asian Economies Country

(GCI) 2006 Ranking (BCI) 2006 Ranking

Bangladesh 99 108

India 43 27

Indonesia 50 35

Malaysia 26 20

Nepal 110 111

Pakistan 91 67

Philippines 71 72

Vietnam 77 82

Business competitiveness has been strongly determined by the prevailing business environment in a country, along with other factors, such as the level of innovation, the availability of university/industry research collaborations, the availability of specialized research and training services, the availability of venture capital, and the dynamism and continuous improvements in company sophistication appropriate to the current stage of a country's development, among other factors. To review how "entrepreneurship" can contribute to productivity and competitiveness of organizations in Asian economies, especially of SMEs, APO designed a survey on "Entrepreneurship Development for Competitive SMEs." The goal was to examine and analyze initiatives and strategies focusing on development of entrepreneurship and business acumen of small enterprises in several different countries and to identify commonalities and differences among the experiences and practices in member countries in order to elicit a common framework at the regional level, resulting in increased competitiveness of Asian SMEs.

The discussion was conducted during the year 2006 in eight member countries: Bangladesh, India, Indonesia, Malaysia, Pakistan, the Philippines, Nepal, and Vietnam.

Commonalities and differences among SME Entrepreneurship Development Initiatives:

A Competitive analysis at the Regional Level

A strong domestic macro-environment with political stability and policy predictability, transparency, and governance, along with a physical and social infrastructure and an efficient Integrated Report legal framework and administrative system, are the basic foundations that will enable the private sector to flourish and will foster entrepreneurship in a country. Additionally, a level playing field, access to finance, and knowledge and skills are indispensable pillars for entrepreneurship.

SME sectors form an integral part of all the Asian economies under review.

Various SME development initiatives and programs have been introduced and implemented in each country at different times, with impacts that are either positive or neutral. A number of these initiatives have indirectly impacted entrepreneurship within SMEs, while some have been directly focused on developing an entrepreneurial culture in the economy. The initiatives, whether direct or indirect or implemented by public- or private-sector institutions, were grouped into six categories.

Promotion of Entrepreneurial Culture

Development of SMEs is strongly linked to the presence of a supportive environment. Initiatives ranging from implementing a receptive regulatory environment to establishing access to technology and finance have been at the forefront. Yet despite these efforts, all the Asian countries in this survey focused on promoting "entrepreneurship" specifically and emphasizing its importance as an independent factor in enhancing competitiveness. The government in each country has played an important role in promoting an entrepreneurial culture. In India,

Malaysia, and the Philippines, private-sector organizations have also made efforts in this regard. Specific promotional initiatives include:

SME Councils/Departments

The Asian governments have established councils/agencies specifically geared toward promoting SME development and entrepreneurial culture in their respective countries. The Ministry of Small Scale Industries (MoSSI) in India, the National SME Council, Small and Medium Industries Development Corporation (SMIDEC) and the Malaysia External Trade Development Corporation (MATRADE) in Malaysia, the Small and Medium Enterprise Development Authority (SMEDA) in Pakistan, the Small and Medium Enterprise Development (SMED) Council in the Philippines, the Bangladesh Small and Cottage Industries Corporation (BSCIC) and subsequently the SME Cell in the Ministry of Industries in Bangladesh, the Ministry of Industries and Trade in Indonesia, the Industrial Promotional Board in Nepal, and the SME Promotion Council in Vietnam have placed SME development at the center of their agendas. In addition to these public-sector departments, private-sector institutions in Malaysia and India are also involved in SME development.

"Entrepreneurship": A Part of the National Action Plan

Entrepreneurship development within SMEs has been made part of the development Action Plan at the national level by India, Malaysia, Pakistan, and the Philippines. Similar initiatives are being taken by Bangladesh and Nepal. Promotion of entrepreneurship among small-scale industries is widely handled through a combination of public- and public-private sector organizations in different countries. In Bangladesh, India, Malaysia, Pakistan, and the Philippines, the Prime Ministers or Presidents have emphasized in speeches the importance of developing entrepreneurship.

The entrepreneurship movement in India began in the 1960s with the establishment of the National Institute of Small Industry Extension Training (NISIET). NISIET was the first institution to develop an Entrepreneurship Development Program (EDP) model in India. At present, the Ministry of Small Scale Industries (MoSSI) and the Ministry of Agro and Rural Industries (ARI) are the two nucleus institutions promoting small-scale industries in India. Under these ministries, the following organizations are responsible for promotion of small-scale enterprises: the Small Industries Development Organization (SIDO), the National Small Industries Corporation (NSIC), the Khadi and Village Industries Commission (KVIC), the Coir Board, and various Entrepreneurship Development for Competitive Small and Medium Enterprises national training institutions. The Ministry of Science and Technology, with its Department of Science and Technology (DST) and its Department of Scientific & Industrial Research (DSIR), is also involved in the promotion of this sector. Several private initiatives by industry associations are also directed toward enterprise promotion. Prominent among them are the Federation of Indian Micro and Small & Medium Enterprises (FISME), the Confederation of Indian Industries (CII), the Associated Chamber of Commerce and Industry (ASSOCHAM), the Federation of Indian Chambers of Commerce and Industry (FICCI), the World Association for Small and Medium Enterprises (WASME), the All India Manufacturers' Organization (AIMO), the Federation of Small Industries of India (FASII), and regional-level industry associations. In the 1990s, entrepreneurship gained momentum in India. Over 700 organizations throughout the country adopted an entrepreneurship strategy to accelerate the start-up of micro, small, and medium enterprises (MSMEs). Presently, under the Ministry of Small Scale Industries (MoSSI), a National Entrepreneurship Development Board (NEDB) devises and recommends policies to promote entrepreneurship and supports surveys and research activities. Grants are provided to reputable organizations engaged in entrepreneurship development for organizing workshops and seminars and conducting research on entrepreneurship development. Academic institutions like NISIET, the National Institute of Entrepreneurship and Small Business Development (NIESBUD), the Indian Institute of Entrepreneurship (IE), and the Entrepreneurship Development Institute of India (EDII), in addition to regional institutions, have utilized these grants for accelerating entrepreneurship activities. The National Manufacturing Competitiveness Council (NMCC) and National Commission for Enterprises in the Unorganized Sector (NCEUS) have recently been instituted to promote, sustain, and strengthen the competitiveness of MSMEs through various activities.

Similarly, in Malaysia the government established the Small and Medium Industries Development Corporation (SMIDEC) in 1996. SMIDEC was tasked with promoting the development of indigenous SMEs that were efficient and competitive as well as capable of producing high value-added, high-quality products and services for the global market. Several programs have been launched since: the Industrial Linkage Programme (ILP); the Technology Development and Acquisition, Skills Development and Upgrading, Market Development, Infrastructure Development, Financial Support, Productivity and Quality Improvement Certification Scheme, the Global Supplier Programme, the Vendor Development Programme, the Head Start 500 Programme, and One District One Industry. Entrepreneurship development among rural SMEs has been promoted by the Malaysia External Trade Development Corporation (MATRADE), which has significantly contributed to the government's effort to promote entrepreneurship, innovation, and competitiveness at the national level, along with e-Perolehan and the Malaysian Franchise Association (MFA).

In the Philippines, the entrepreneurial mindset surfaced during the 1970s. Its importance became evident with the appointment of a Presidential Adviser on Entrepreneurship and the establishment of private institutions such as the Small Enterprise Research and Development Foundation (SERDEF), the Philippine Business for Social Progress (PBSP), and Chambers of Commerce such as the Philippine Chamber of Commerce and Industry (PCCI) and the Employers' Confederation of the Philippines (ECOP). SMEs have been positively identified as an important strategy for creating new jobs and hastening the economic recovery and growth of the country. Thus, in support of the government's agenda of tripling the number of loans made available to SMEs and creating six million jobs in six years by giving more opportunities to entrepreneurs, the SMED Council, through the Department of Trade and Industry (DTI), in 2004 launched the SME Development Plan 2004–10. The Plan aims to make the SME sector the key shaper of the country's economic growth by 2010. It is a six-year strategic development plan geared towards building the capabilities of both SMEs and SME support organizations by providing relevant services and assistance to enhance their competitiveness so as to significantly increase the contributions of SMEs to the country's economic growth.

The Industrial Enterprise Act of 1961 was the first government initiative undertaken for SME development in Nepal. The tenth plan (2002–07) outlined the broad objectives, indicators, and outcomes in the industry sector. Entrepreneurship development programs are also based on this plan and are implemented under the Ministry of Industry, Commerce and Supplies (MoICs).

Various organizations involved in SME development, both public and private, carry out entrepreneurship promotional activities as and when necessary. The Department of Cottage and Small Industry (DCSI), operating in 27 districts, the Cottage and Small Industry Development Board (CSIDB), operating in 48 districts, the Industrial Enterprise Development Institute (IEDI), the Federation of Nepalese Chambers of Commerce and Industry (FNCCI), the Federation of Nepalese Cottage and Small Industries(FNCSI), and various commodity associations and NGOs in the private sector undertake promotional activities. In 2002, the Industrial Development Prospective Plan—Vision 2020—was introduced, with the goal of promoting entrepreneurship, innovation, and competitiveness at the national level.

SME development became one of the core agenda items of the government of Pakistan in 1999 to create employment opportunities, reduce poverty, and improve overall economic development. Various initiatives were undertaken thereafter to promote SME development. Specific organizations such as the Small and Medium Enterprise Development Authority (SMEDA) and the SME Bank were established or restructured to promote and develop the entrepreneurial culture within SMEs. However, "entrepreneurship" development within SMEs has become more pertinent with the introduction of the government's Medium Term Development Framework 2005–10 and the subsequent SME Policy. According to the policy statement, "The government is committed to developing the SME sector to achieve higher economic growth and maximize creation of jobs to alleviate poverty. SMEs will be made more competitive by through the provision of a favorable business environment, greater access to formal financing and support in technical upgrades, human resource development, marketing, and innovation. The government will facilitate establishment of new businesses by developing policies that help in realizing the entrepreneurial potential of the people of Pakistan." The policy includes five recommendations for developing entrepreneurship within the SME sector, ranging from introducing entrepreneurship as a subject in educational institutions to competitions at the national level to setting up business incubators.

Small Business Entrepreneurs Awards and Quality Awards

Small Business Entrepreneurs and Quality Awards have been successfully introduced in

India. The Ministry of Cooperative and Entrepreneurship Development and SMIDEC have introduced Entrepreneurship and Quality Awards in Malaysia. Additionally, Master Pack Sdn. Bhd and Samsung SDI (M) Sdn. Bhd (private-sector organizations in Malaysia) have introduced a Small Business Entrepreneur Award. Quality awards have also been successfully launched in Indonesia.

The Philippines has been successful in launching various awards for SMEs, focusing on entrepreneurship: -

1. Presidential Awards for Outstanding SME Graduates. The Outstanding SME Graduates are entrepreneurs who have excelled in their respective fields not only through government assistance but also through their own initiatives to improve their competitiveness.
2. Golden Shell Awards. These biennial awards are the highest award/recognition given by the Department of Trade and Industry, through the Center for International Trade Expositions and Missions (CITEM), to Filipino companies (exporters) for excellence in exports. Separate awards are given to manufacturing and service exporters on the basis of design, manufacturing/service, and marketing excellence. Awards are also given for Entrepreneurship Development for Competitive Small and Medium Enterprises introducing a new product (Rising Star), rural development, and significantly impacting the country's exports.

3. Philippine Quality Award (PQA). The Philippine Quality Award is the highest level of national recognition for exemplary organizational performance. In addition to quality excellence, awards are also given for Mastery in Quality Management, Proficiency in Quality Management, and Commitment to Quality Management.

Likewise in Pakistan, private-sector institutions have been successful in promoting entrepreneurship by launching the following awards:

1. Shell Tameer's Young Business Start-up Award. This award recognizes the efforts of young entrepreneurs through business start-up awards on an annual basis.
2. LUMS' Young Entrepreneur of the Year, Female Entrepreneur of the Year, and Small Business of the Year Awards. Each year an individual is honored through induction into the "Hall of Fame." These individuals are selected from among those who have started from scratch and achieved outstanding success in business as a result of their entrepreneurial spirit.
3. President's Quality Award. This award is given on an annual basis by the National Productivity Organization for SMEs excelling in productivity and quality.
4. FPCCI's Best Lady Exporter Gold. This award is conferred on a woman entrepreneur who in the judgment of the Federation of Pakistani Chambers of Commerce & Industry has achieved the best export performance during the year.

In Nepal, no quality or entrepreneurship award has been designed as yet at the national level. However, the Export Promotion Board annually honors the "Exporter of the Year."

Similarly, the **Women Entrepreneurs Association of Nepal** (WEAN) gives awards to women entrepreneurs, while the Cottage and Small Industry Development Board (CSIDB) recognizes a "Successful Entrepreneur" during the national trade fair exhibitions.

Promotion of Technology and Technopreneurs

The National Science and Technology Entrepreneurship Development Board (NSTEDB) under the Ministry of Science and Technology in India operates the Techno-Entrepreneur Promotion Program (TEPP), which focuses on promoting, supporting, and assisting individual innovators in becoming technology-based entrepreneurs. The National Research Development Corporation (NRDC), the Council of Scientific and Industrial Research (CSIR), the Department of Science and Technology, and the Central Food Technological Research Institute have implemented successful programs for technological innovation in SMEs. In Malaysia, technological innovation has been successfully handled by MATRADE. Promotion of technology and Technopreneurs in Pakistan is being undertaken by the National University of Sciences and Technology (NUST), which has been providing an opportunity to potential entrepreneurs from the general public,students, and NUST faculty to incubate their technology-based companies at its Technology Incubation Center (TIC). In addition, the Pakistan Software Export Board (PSEB) promotes Technopreneurs by facilitating the establishment of IT businesses in Pakistan.

14

Promotion of Women Entrepreneurship

Women entrepreneurship development has been a focus in many Asian countries. Promotion of women entrepreneurship in India is being undertaken by not-for-profit/private-sector organizations such as AWAKE, ALEAP, and CWEI; these institutions focus primarily on counseling, training, handholding, giving guidance on finance, organizing exhibitions, and peer group support. The Consortium of Women Entrepreneurs of India (CWEI) has also started networking with women entrepreneurs in other countries to market the products of India internationally. In Malaysia, women entrepreneurship is promoted by the Ministry of Women and Social Affairs, and the Women's SME Association of Malaysia. Similarly, in the Philippines, in addition to the various microfinance programs, the Women Workers Employment and Entrepreneurship Development (WEED) program of the Department of Labor and Employment (DOLE) aims to strengthen women entrepreneurs by providing a "Training-Cum-Production" scheme which consists of Entrepreneurship Development Training (EDT) and Appropriate Skills Training (AST).

A major entrepreneurial venture of the Bangladesh Small and Cottage Industries Corporation (BSCIC) has been conducted under the Women Entrepreneurship Development Programme (WEDP). Since the early 1980s, WEDP has created more than 40,000 female-headed establishments. BSCIC's program has undoubtedly made a significant contribution to the emergence of small and micro businesses in Bangladesh. Four women's trade bodies are working for women entrepreneurship development.

Indonesia has promoted women entrepreneurship since 1984. The program aims to improve the role of small industry as a mover for economic activity in the region, so that it can increase businesses and working opportunities for the community and also help the number of women entrepreneurs grow in the various regions of the country. The goal of the program is to establish new women entrepreneurs in groups (at least 20 women–group businesses per year) and to create small industrial business units (at least 400 units per year). From 1984 to 2005 the program established 743 groups of women industrial businesses in all regions of the country. These include 226 groups in food, 235 groups in textiles, and 282 groups in small craft industries.

The Women Entrepreneurs Association of Nepal (WEAN), a nonprofit and nongovernmental organization, is the main organization involved in empowering women through enterprise promotion. It offers training, marketing assistance, credit, networking, and other extension services to urban and rural women entrepreneurs. DCSI and CSIDB, the major organizations involved in entrepreneurship development in Nepal, conduct different types of skill development training targeting women entrepreneurs. The Women Development Division implements various capacity-building programs for women in all 75 districts of Nepal. The Women Development Training Centre targets only women in its skill development training. The Micro Enterprise Development Program of the United Nations Development Programme (MEDEP/UNDP) and the Rural Enterprise Assistance Program of the Industrial Enterprise Development Institute (REAP/IEDI) have given priority to women and other disadvantaged groups in their microenterprise programs. Women entrepreneurs committees have been established under the FNCCI and FNCSI to promote women entrepreneurship.

Women entrepreneurship development has received much attention in Pakistan over the last five years. SMEDA has established a separate Women Entrepreneurship Development Cell, while an independent Women Chamber of Commerce and Industry (WCCI) has also been formed. In addition, a number of chambers of commerce and industry have women standing committees to promote women entrepreneurship. The Export Promotion Bureau (EBP) has facilitated the creation of WEXNET, an online networking forum for women, where women entrepreneurs interact with each other and can also exhibit their products in exhibitions organized by the EPB. Women in Technology (WIT), a project of the Ministry of Information

Technology and Communication, promotes technology-related education, career counseling, entrepreneurship, and empowerment of women entrepreneurs. The Shell Tameer program also supports new women enterprises.

Promotion of Youth Entrepreneurship

To promote entrepreneurship among students, linkages are spearheaded by the appointed Philippines Presidential Adviser on Entrepreneurship and supported by the PCCI, the Anvil Business Club, and the Chinese–Filipino Business Club. Further, Philippine Emerging Startups Open (PESO), a student organization at the Massachusetts Institute of Technology (MIT), has recently been incorporated in the Philippines through the initiative of a group of educators, Entrepreneurship Development for Competitive Small and Medium Enterprises industry professionals, and venture capitalists. Seeking start-ups in IT as well as in non-IT fields,

PESO works to stimulate powerful new ideas and identify ideas with potential for successful incubation and commercialization, to promote productive interactions between the academic, industry, and investment sectors, to inspire and empower young people to take the path of entrepreneurship by giving them access to proper resources, role models, and mentors, and to foster innovation, excellence, and professionalism in the entrepreneurship process. In Pakistan, youth entrepreneurship is being promoted by educational institutions like Lahore University of Management Sciences (LUMS), the Institute of Business Administration (IBA), and the Shell Tameer program. A number of business and management schools facilitate internships to enable students to gain practical experience in business management.

National Entrepreneurship Profile

The SMIDEC and National Productivity Council (NPC) in Malaysia have evolved to promote the Malay Entrepreneurship Profile for SMEs, while NISIET has developed a profile for Indian entrepreneurs. The Bangladesh Small and Cottage Industries Corporation (BSCIC) has been working in SME development for the past 35 years and has developed an Entrepreneurship Profile for small and cottage industries resulting in a number of success stories.

Nepal has also taken the initiative to develop an Entrepreneurship Profile based on the general characteristics of its entrepreneurs.

Regulation and Policies

A "level playing field" is indispensable for entrepreneurship and SMEs to develop and flourish in any economy. A level playing field can be created with the effective implementation of a fair and predictable system of rules and enforcement mechanisms. A transparent regulatory environment and policy framework ensures that entrepreneurs are facilitated in entering the market, operating a business venture, and exiting from the market. It supports entrepreneurs in gaining access to markets and financing and infrastructure facilities. To support the development of a favorable regulatory environment, the following initiatives have been taken in different Asian countries.

Policy/Regulation for SME Development

The MoSSI, Ministry of Finance, and Ministry of Planning in India have developed the policies and framework for SME development in that country, while the MoST has designed the technological development policy. MoSSI and ARI have also developed policies for increasing SMEs' access to markets and financial services. Similarly, in Malaysia, the Ministry of Cooperative and Entrepreneurship Development has formulated the regulations for SME development. SMIDEC has devised the SME framework. Technological development within Malaysian SMEs is supported through policies devised by SMIDEC, SIRIM (Standard and Industrial Research Institute of Malaysia), the technology agency MARA, and especially the Malaysian Technology Development Corporation Sdn. Bhd in the private sector, which has introduced the Technology Acquisition Fund. The Ministry of Science and Technology focuses on regulations for introducing ICT in the country. Malaysia has also introduced policies to facilitate SMEs' access to markets. These policies have increased the cost-competitiveness of locally produced products. The basic policy of the Philippines for SMEs is outlined in the Magna Carta for Small Enterprises, enacted in 1991 and amended in 1997. The Act declares that it is the policy of the state to promote, support, strengthen, and encourage the growth and development of SMEs in all productive sectors of the economy. The goals under the Magna Carta include creating an enabling favorable business environment, improving access to financing, providing adequate business support, providing training on entrepreneurship and worker skills, providing linkages between SMEs and large firms, and working in partnership with the private sector.

In continuation of the Pakistan government's Poverty Reduction Strategy, the Medium Term Development Framework 2005–10 has emphasized the development of the SMEs. Based on the same strategy, the Small and Medium Enterprise

Development Authority (SMEDA), with the collaboration of the private sector, developed a comprehensive SME Policy in 2006 that focuses on five major aspects: business environment, access to finance, human resource development, support for technology upgrades and marketing, and entrepreneurship development.

In 2005, the Ministry of Industries of the government of Bangladesh formulated the comprehensive Industrial Policy 2005, putting special emphasis on developing small and medium enterprises as a thrust sector for balanced and sustainable industrial development and to help deal with the challenges of the free-market economy and globalization. The efforts of the MOI are being supported through the technical assistance of the Asian Development Bank under the SME Sector Development Program. The policy focuses on entrepreneurship development among SMEs. The government also has a Science and Technology Policy to support technological development in the SME sector.

Considering the importance of the SME sector in national economic development, the government of Vietnam adopted Decree 90/2001/ND–CP for SME development on 23 November 2001. This is considered to be the first legal framework for SME development policies, covering SME definition, support programs, support agencies, and support policies— i.e., investment support through financial and credit measures, establishment of a Credit Guarantee Fund, development of industrial zones and clusters, measures for market expansion, export support, training in human resources development, provision of information on production focused business through the Internet and print publications, and business incubators. Further, the introduction and application of the Enterprise Law (2000) has created a transparent environment for business activities and is considered a milestone of administrative reform, significantly improving the consistency, unity, transparency, and equality of the legal framework for business.

This has led to a "level playing field" for different types of enterprises and has increased the development of economic sectors in general and SMEs in particular.

The government of Nepal formulated the Industrial Enterprise Act in 1992. Incentives, facilities, and other concessions are provided based on the nature of business, location, number of employment, and other criteria. Provision is made for additional incentives to those industries, as a national priority. The Foreign Investment and Technology Transfer Act 1992 was adopted to attract foreign investment and technology transfer.

Registration/Launching of SMEs

Registration of SMEs is still a cumbersome procedure in the Philippines. Entrepreneurs can expect to go through 11 steps to launch a business over 48 days on average, at a cost equal to 20.3% of gross national income (GNI) per capita—approximately US$237.12. They must deposit at least 2.0% of GNI per capita in a bank to obtain a business registration number.

Similarly, registration of firms is also arduous in Nepal. Under the Industrial Enterprise Act of Nepal, SMEs must be registered in the Department of Cottage and Small Industry (DCSI) or the

Department of Industry based on the size of their capital investment. However, local governments are authorized to collect taxes and register industries established in their areas. Moreover, an Initial Environment Examination (IEE) is required, along with other documents. Advance permission is required if the industry is related to health, pollution, or arms/ammunition. This has created confusion in matters of legal status and regulatory jurisdiction between the central and the local governments; hence, the provisions are seen as burdensome by entrepreneurs.

The Securities and Exchange Commission of Pakistan has issued regulations and procedures for the formation of Single Member companies to promote registration of SMEs.

Moreover, the corporate registration offices have been strengthened to facilitate the incorporation of SMEs. An "availability of name" search, sample documents, the fee structure, and the procedure for registration are available on the SEC's website, thus saving time and simplifying Entrepreneurship Development for Competitive Small and Medium Enterprises the registration process. However, further strengthening of the system is still necessary, in addition to the promotion of incorporation as an alternative to partnerships and sole proprietorships. Similarly, regional industry departments and the Registrar of Companies in India and SMIDEC in Malaysia have been successful in promoting registration of SMEs. Business establishment regulations in these countries are comparatively simple, which encourages SMEs to register as formal business organizations. Laws regarding registration of SMEs have also been developed in Bangladesh. However, no policies for launching SMEs are available in Nepal, Indonesia, or Vietnam.

Bankruptcy Laws

Bankruptcy laws to simplify the closing of non-competitive enterprises have been successfully developed in India by the Board of Industrial Finance and Reconstruction (BIFR) with the support of the Federation of the Indian Chambers of Commerce and Industry. Similarly, in Malaysia these laws have been enacted successfully by the Ministry of Finance. In the Philippines, bankruptcy laws are weaker. It takes 5.7 years to complete the procedure, as estimated by bankruptcy lawyers. Delays result from legal derailment tactics that parties to the bankruptcy may use—in particular, the extension of response periods or appeals. The cost of bankruptcy proceedings is

38% of the estate. Beyond procedural improvements, which have been attempted, the Philippine bankruptcy/insolvency system needs to be rationalized and updated. The current legal framework is a mixture of outdated and inconsistent laws and judicial pronouncements. Similarly, a bankruptcy law exists in Bangladesh, but its effectiveness needs to be reviewed. In Nepal, provisions related to closure, liquidation, and bankruptcy are mentioned in the Industrial Enterprise Act.

In Vietnam, the Bankruptcy Law 2004 has simplified bankruptcy proceedings and regulates different kinds of applicable procedures for debtors in bankruptcy. However, the law has some limitations. For example, business households and individuals are not eligible to declare bankruptcy, and secured creditors are not entitled to file petitions to start bankruptcy proceedings.

The SME policy of Pakistan recommends the strengthening of the regulatory framework for the development of SMEs. Bankruptcy laws are an important component of the regulations, which need to be developed and enforced with a dedicated judicial process specifically for the SMEs. In Pakistan, a draft bankruptcy law to support SMEs as well as individuals and entrepreneurs has been prepared and is expected to be passed shortly.

Labor Laws for SMEs

The Ministry of Labor has devised policies for protecting the rights of workers in SMEs in

India. Similarly, DOLE, through the National Wages and Productivity Commission (NWPC), and the Regional Tripartite Wages and Productivity Boards (RTWPBs) in the Philippines developed certain measures in 2005 which have shown a proactive stance and sensitivity to the needs of workers without sacrificing the competitiveness of business enterprises. Under the SME policy in Pakistan, labor laws are being reviewed to devise measures for the facilitation of SMEs.

In Nepal, labor laws apply to businesses that employ more than 10 workers. Various provisions such as minimum salaries, working hours, and formation of unions are included for the protection of workers' rights.

SME Financing Regulations

Minimum lending guidelines have been formulated for lending to SMEs in Malaysia. The Nepal Rastra Bank (Central Bank) has made some provisions to finance cottage and small industries through different banks. However, these programs and policies, designed to finance micro and small enterprises, have not been adequate to address the needs of small and medium entrepreneurs. The State Bank of Pakistan (Central Bank) has issued independent prudential.

15
Women Entrepreneurship: All Women Are Endowed With Innate Power

That Can Make Them Successful Entrepreneurs

Women Entrepreneurship Is Inherent and Also A Natural Process:

Maternity is a creative capacity involving risk of life. Maternal instincts generate enormous strength and determination that drive the fear away from them. Courageousness and determination that generate at the time of maternity are in born. These characters generate within themselves and not come from elsewhere. Women empowerment becomes reality by nurturing their innate qualities of entrepreneurship.

Women Is Naturally Endowed With The Qualities Of Entrepreneurship:

My second sister got married, and we are quite happy for she was blessed with good husband and in-laws. However, our happiness short lived as she had miscarriages. Every **couple dream of children** in their initial days of marital life, elders also eagerly awaits the grandchildren. Their happiness gets delayed for months and years, and they could not conquer the Frustration and anxiety. The problem diagnosed was the incompetent cervix. We feared a lot when she got Pregnancy again. We approached the Senior Gynecologist who assured that the problem could be resolved by stitching up the cervix. With this advice hope was regenerated. After three months doctor stitched up the cervix and advised complete bed rest under her supervision in the hospital.

From that time onwards **she was on bed for more than 5 months. She has undergone trauma of immovable life.** We are very anxious. However, she displayed a lot of Patience and courage. At last there was a sign of relief among all the members of the family, as she gave birth to a baby girl "bless y". The way my sister demonstrated her patience and maturity surprised us. I realized that women are naturally blessed with the qualities of entrepreneurship. **I also realized that women entrepreneurship and women empowerment would be the realities of tomorrow.** This is a usual phenomenon in the life of any woman.

Every woman undergoes a risk of life to bring life into this world. Women do not deny motherhood on the plea of risk is involved. Their maternal instincts overcome the thoughts of risk to life. **Women have the innate ability to face the risk of life with firm courage.** This is an essential quality for Entrepreneurship. Women entrepreneurship is therefore, a natural process for women. Encouragement of women entrepreneurs are the only solution for women empowerment.

Entrepreneurship Is Like Giving Birth To A Child:

Entrepreneurship is like giving birth to a child. The Women's Love of child overcomes the risk of life. The entrepreneur overcomes the risk of loss with the passion of entrepreneurship. Bringing life by the women is experiencing the inborn creative capacity. When you are creating an enterprise you are experiencing your creative capacity.

Women Entrepreneurship Can Only Bring About Women Empowerment:

When **women bring life** into this world, it contributes to the society. When an entrepreneur creates an enterprise it generates employment, create wealth. Entrepreneurship is a prerequisite for the development of any nation. Hence the contributions of women entrepreneurs are a prerequisite for nation building. Women entrepreneurship, women empowerment and nation building are therefore, synonymous.

Women are naturally endowed with the emotions of love. This positive energy could be used managing human resources efficiently. All the women have all the resources to manage an enterprise. Women entrepreneurship can only bring about women empowerment. Social entrepreneurship can eliminate the ignorance and poverty.

Social entrepreneurship

Social entrepreneurship describes an entrepreneurial venture that aims to achieve a desired social change.

Business entrepreneurs typically measure performance in profit and return, but social entrepreneurs also take into account a positive return to society. Social entrepreneurship typically furthers broad social, cultural, and environmental goals and is commonly associated with the voluntary and not-for-profit sectors. Profit can at times also be a consideration for certain companies or other enterprises.

Social entrepreneurship practiced in a world or international context is called international social entrepreneurship.

History

The terms social entrepreneur and social entrepreneurship were used first in the literature on social change in the 1960s and 1970s. The terms came into widespread use in the 1980s and 1990s, promoted by Bill Drayton the founder of Ashoka: Innovators for the Public and others such as Charles Lead beater. From the 1950s to the 1990s Michael Young was a leading promoter of social enterprise and in the 1980s was described by Professor Daniel Bell at Harvard as 'the world's most successful entrepreneur of social enterprises' because of his role in creating more than sixty new organizations worldwide, including the School for Social Entrepreneurs (SSE) which exists in the UK, Australia and Canada and which supports individuals to realize their potential and to establish, scale and sustain, social enterprises and social businesses. Another notable British social entrepreneur is Andrew Mawson OBE, who was given a peerage in 2007 because of his regeneration work including the Bromley by Bow Centre in East London.

Although the terms are relatively new, social entrepreneurs and social entrepreneurship can be found throughout history. A list of a few historically noteworthy people whose work exemplifies classic "social entrepreneurship" might include Florence Nightingale, founder of the first nursing school and developer of modern nursing practices; Robert Owen, founder of the cooperative movement; and Vinoba Bhave, founder of India's Land Gift Movement. During the nineteenth and twentieth century's some of the most successful social entrepreneurs effectively straddled the civic, governmental, and business worlds – promoting ideas that were taken up by mainstream public services in welfare, schools, and health care.

Current practice

One well-known contemporary social entrepreneur is Muhammad Yunus, founder and manager of Grameen Bank and its growing family of social venture businesses, who was awarded a Nobel Peace Prize in 2006. The work of Yunus and Grameen echoes a theme among modern day social entrepreneurs that emphasizes the enormous synergies and benefits when business principles are unified with social ventures. In some countries - including Bangladesh - social entrepreneurs have filled the spaces left by a relatively small state. In other countries - particularly in Europe and South America - they have tended to work more closely with public organizations at both the national and local level.

Today, nonprofits and non-governmental organizations, foundations, governments, and individuals also play the role to promote, fund, and advise social entrepreneurs around the planet. A growing number of colleges and universities are establishing programs focused on educating and training social entrepreneurs.

The George Foundation's Women's Empowerment program empowers women by providing education, cooperative farming, vocational training, savings planning, and business development. In 2006 the cooperative farming program, Baldev Farms, was the second largest banana grower in South India with 250 acres (1.0 km2) under cultivation. Profits from the farm are used for improving the economic status of the workers and for running the other charitable activities of the foundation.

Some have created for-profit and for-a-difference organizations. A recent example is Vikram Akula, the McKinsey alumnus who started a microlending venture, SKS Microfinance, in villages of Indian state of Andhra Pradesh. Although this venture is for profit, it has initiated a sharp social change amongst poor women from villages. Other examples of social entrepreneurs in Healthcare in India is Ramanujan Bose Awardee Dr Akash S Rajpal, Founder of Ekohealth has been working in India in the field of healthcare against Fee splitting and creating a unique ethical facilitation and aggregation services for healthcare providers and price comparison services for patients and help them reduce health care costs.

There are continuing arguments over precisely who counts as a social entrepreneur. The lack of consensus on the definition of social entrepreneurship means that other disciplines are often confused with and mistakenly associated with social entrepreneurship. Philanthropists, social activists, environmentalists, and other socially-oriented practitioners are referred to as social entrepreneurs. It is important to set the function of social entrepreneurship apart from other socially oriented activities and identify the boundaries within which social entrepreneurs operate. Some have advocated restricting the term to founders of organizations that primarily rely on earned income – meaning income earned directly from paying consumers. Others have extended this to include contracted work for public authorities, while still others include grants and donations. This argument is unlikely to be resolved soon. Peter Drucker, for example, once wrote that there was nothing so entrepreneurial as creating a new university: yet in most developed countries the majority of university funding comes from the state.

Organizations such as Ashoka: Innovators for the Public, the Skoll Foundation, the Omidyar Network, the Schwab Foundation for Social Entrepreneurship, Athgo, New Profit Inc., National Social Entrepreneurship Forum, and Echoing Green among others, focus on highlighting these hidden change-makers who are scattered throughout the world. Ashoka's Changemakers "open sourcing social solutions" initiative Changemakers uses an online platform for what it calls collaborative competitions to build communities of practice around pressing issues.

The North American organizations tend to have a strongly individualistic stance focused on a handful of exceptional leaders, while others in Asia and Europe emphasize more how social entrepreneurs work within teams, networks, and movements for change. The Skoll Foundation, created by eBay's first president, Jeff Skoll, makes capacity-building "mezzanine level" grants to social entrepreneurial organizations that already have reached a certain level of impact, connects them through the annual Skoll World Forum and Social Edge, the Foundation's online community, and highlights their work through partnerships with the Sundance Institute, Frontline World, NewsHour with Jim Lehrer, and other film and broadcast outlets. Skoll also supports the field of social entrepreneurship, including through Skoll's founding of the Skoll Centre for Social Entrepreneurship at the Said Business School at Oxford University. Examples of social entrepreneurial business in the USA include NIKA Water Company, which sells bottled water in the USA and uses 100% of its profits to bring clean water to those in the developing world, as well as Newman's Own which donates 100% of its profits to support various educational charities.

Youth social entrepreneurship is an increasingly common approach to engaging youth voice in solving social problems. Youth organizations and programs promote these efforts through a variety of incentives to young people. One such program is Young Social Pioneers, which invests in the power and promise of Australia's young leaders. The program, which is an initiative of The Foundation for Young Australians, strengthens supports and celebrates the role of young people in creating positive change in their communities.

Fast Company Magazine annually publishes a list of the twenty-five best social entrepreneurs, which the magazine defines as organizations "using the disciplines of the corporate world to tackle daunting social problems." In 2009, Business Week followed suit, publishing a review of America's twenty-five most promising social entrepreneurs, defined as "enterprising individuals who apply business practices to solving societal problems."

The internet and social networking websites have been pivotal resources for the success and collaboration of many Social Entrepreneurs. Captain Edward Zellem of www.AfghanProverbs.

com has been working with Film Annex's Afghan Development project as an example individual social entrepreneurship that merges his work with the study of languages and culture into the film platform at Film Annex. These media allow ideas to be heard by broader audiences, help networks and investors to develop globally, and achieve their goals with little or no start-up capital. The US-based nonprofit Zidisha leverages the recent spread of internet and mobile technologies in developing technologies to provide an eBay-style microlending platform where disadvantaged individuals in developing countries can interact directly with individual "peer-to-peer" lenders worldwide, sourcing small business loans at lower cost than has ever before been possible in most developing countries. In addition the internet allows for the pooling of design resources using open source principles. For example, the rise of open-source appropriate technology as a sustainable development paradigm enables people all over the world to collaborate on solving local problems just as open source software development leverages collaboration.

Corporate social entrepreneurship

A **corporate social entrepreneur** (CSE) is defined as "an employee of the firm who operates in a socially entrepreneurial manner; identifying opportunities for and/ or championing socially responsible activity; in addition to helping the firm achieve its business targets. The CSE operates regardless of an organizational context that is pre-disposed towards corporate social responsibility (CSR). This is because the CSE is driven by their dominant self-transcendent (concerned with the welfare of others) as opposed to their self-enhancement personal values. Consequently, the CSE does not necessarily have a formal socially responsible job role, nor do they necessarily have to be in a senior management position to progress their socially responsible agenda."

Relevance

The notion of the CSE primarily relates to the field of corporate social responsibility. It is thus relevant to both practitioners and scholars of business and management and more specifically to the fields of business ethics; organizational; entrepreneurship; human resource management and business strategy. Moreover, the concept is inherently linked with the notion of personal values: in itself, a field of study from sociology; anthropology and social psychology. Furthermore, due to the concept's associations with ideas about agency, this also means that this topic connects with moral philosophy. Such complexity reflects the inter-disciplinary nature of the field of corporate social responsibility.

Background

The notion of the CSE first emerged in 2002 from a conceptual working paper which was published in the Hull University Business School Research Memoranda Series. In that paper, it was argued that CSR can also be motivated by an altruistic impulse driven by managers' personal values, in addition to the more obvious economic and macro political drivers for CSR. This reflected the traditional philosophical and business ethics debate regarding moral agency. This paper was followed by a U.K. conference paper which highlighted the importance of managerial discretion in CSR and was published the next year in the Journal of Business Ethics. In this latter paper, the concept of "entrepreneurial discretion" as an overlooked antecedent of CSR was mooted.

Consequently, the term corporate social entrepreneur was first coined in a paper that was presented at the 17th Annual European Business Ethics Network Conference, in June 2004. Here, the term Corporate Social Entrepreneur was first defined and differentiated from the different types of entrepreneurs: the 'regular' executive entrepreneur; the intrapreneur; the policy entrepreneur and the public or social entrepreneur. Initially, the concept was discussed in relation to managers. However, it was soon widened to include employees at any level of the firm, regardless of their formally appointed status. To be a CSE you do not necessarily have to be a manager. Seniority is not necessary, but, of course, it helps.

Hemingway's concept of the CSE emerged as a result of her own personal experience working as a marketing executive in the corporate world and it has also been the subject of some exploratory empirical investigation. It was also inspired by Wood, who had previously referred to "Ethical training, cultural background, preferences...and life experiences... that motivate human behavior"; thereby supporting Trevino's conceptual "Interactionist" model of ethical decision making in organizations. Trevino's model included both individual and situational moderators, to combine with the individual's stage of cognitive moral development, to produce either ethical or unethical behaviour. And whilst studies existed regarding the activities of environmental champions at work or other change leaders, none of these studies specifically examined the role of employees' personal values in entrepreneurial discretion with regard to corporate social responsibility (CSR).

Thus, the connection between philosophical ideas of moral character as an influence for corporate social responsibility (CSR) and linked to the psychological notion of prosocial behavior, provides a different focus from the more commonly discussed structural drivers for CSR, i.e., business strategy in the form of public relations activity; encouragement from government or organizational context.

Business ethics perspective

Significantly, whilst the social entrepreneur and corporate social entrepreneur are united in their quest to create social value: a business ethics perspective encourages us to ask the question 'For what end?' Here business ethics is useful, as it uses intellectual frameworks to encourage us to think deeply about means and ends. For example, the idea of the CSE creating social value which benefits both the corporation and society is known as 'enlightened self-interest'. Alternatively, a deontological viewpoint frames acts of socially responsible behaviour as driven by the individual's sense of duty to society, which may be viewed in terms of altruism. Altruism is of course very difficult to support empirically, although there have been many studies of prosocial behaviour and support for the notion of self-transcendent personal values in social psychology.

Threat or opportunity

All this leads us to the inherent complexity surrounding the subject of CSR, regarding its connection to stakeholder theory and its "essentially contested" nature. So, whilst some studies have shown a positive relationship between CSR and financial performance, others are currently investigating the notion of non-market performance [2].Consequently, the notion of the Corporate Social Entrepreneur is equally controversial: not solely due to the arguments about the role of business and whether or not CSR helps financial performance; but also because the concept of employee discretion has been identified as a key factor regarding a social orientation at work, or, a moral character (in the ancient philosophical sense). And whilst the possibility of unethical behaviour is also acknowledged as an outcome of discretion and agency: corporate irresponsibility which has been the traditional focus in the study of business ethics, is regarded as insufficient and only the starting point, if the quest is for organisations to develop a socially responsible organizational context. This is of particular relevance in the wake of the global financial crisis caused by financial irregularities and lapses in corporate governance and personal integrity.

List of social entrepreneurs

A **social entrepreneur** is an entrepreneur who works to increase social capital, often by founding humanitarian organizations.

Historical examples of leading social entrepreneurs

- Susan B. Anthony (U.S.) - Fought for women's rights in the United States, including the right to control property, and helped spearhead adoption of the 19th amendment.
- Vinoba Bhave (India) - Founder and leader of the Land Gift Movement, he caused the redistribution of more than 7,000,000 acres (28,000 km^2) of land to aid India's untouchables and landless. Mahatma Gandhi described him as his mentor.
- David Brower (U.S.) - Environmentalist and conservationist, he served as the Sierra Club's first executive director and built it into a worldwide network for environmental issues. He also founded Friends of the Earth, the League of Conservation Voters and The Earth Island Institute.
- Akhtar Hameed Khan (Pakistan) - Founder of grassroots movement for rural communities Comilla Model, and low-cost sanitation programmes (Orangi Pilot Project) for squatter settlements.
- Maria Montessori (Italy) - Developed the Montessori approach to early childhood education.
- John Muir (U.S.) - Naturalist and conservationist, he established the National Park System and helped found The Sierra Club.
- Florence Nightingale (UK) - Founder of modern nursing, she established the first school for nurses and fought to improve hospital conditions.
- Frederick Law Olmsted (U.S.) - Creator of major urban parks, including Rock Creek Park in Washington DC,

Central Park in NYC, and Mount Royal Park in Montreal, he is generally considered to have developed the profession of landscape architecture in America.

- Gifford Pinchot (U.S.) - Champion of the forest as a multiple use environment, he helped found the Yale School of Forestry and created the U.S. Forest Service, serving as its first chief.
- Friedrich Wilhelm Raiffeisen (Germany) - Pioneer of the rural bond of association as a substitute for collateral in microfinance, and a principal founder of the credit union and cooperative bank sectors that now form a major segment of the European banking system.
- Margaret Sanger (U.S.) - Founder of the Planned Parenthood Federation of America, she led the movement for family planning efforts around the world.
- John Woolman (U.S.) - Led U.S. Quakers to voluntarily emancipate all their slaves between 1758 and 1800, his work also influenced the British Society of Friends, a major force behind the British decision to ban slaveholding. Quakers, of course, became a major force in the U.S. abolitionist movement as well as a key part of the infrastructure of the Underground Railroad.

Present day social entrepreneurs

- Ibrahim Abouleish (Egypt) - Founder of SEKEM, a biodynamic agricultural corporation, alternative medicine, and educational center located outside of Cairo.
- Gennady Alferenko (Russia) - Founder of the Foundation for Social Inventions and Foundation for Social Innovations.
- Ela Bhatt (India) - Founder of the Self-Employed Women's Association (SEWA) and the SEWA Cooperative Bank in Gujarat.
- Nathaniel Dunigan (Uganda). -- Founder of Aidchild; Reynolds Fellow in Social Entrepreneurship at the Center

for Public Leadership at the Harvard Kennedy School; the Dammeyer Fellow in Global Education Leadership at the University of San Diego; and Cordes Fellow at the Opportunity Collaboration 2012.

- Bill Drayton (U.S.) - Founded Ashoka, Youth Venture, and Get America Working!
- Marian Wright Edelman (U.S.) - Founder and president of the Children's Defense Fund (CDF) and advocate for disadvantaged Americans and children.
- Dr. Abraham M. George (India) - Founder of The George Foundation (TGF).
- Pamela Hartigan (U.S.) - Founding partner of Volans Ventures and founding managing director of the Schwab Foundation
- Alan Khazei (U.S.) - Co-Founder of City Year, a leading national service program.
- Dr. Verghese Kurien (India) - Founder of the AMUL Dairy Project.
- Jamie Oliver (U.K.) - TV chef who campaigned to improve children's diet at school. He also trained disadvantaged young people to become chefs. He created a restaurant - a social enterprise - called fifteen which employed these newly trained youngsters. Fifteen is now a global chain of four restaurants.
- Bunker Roy (India) - Founder of Barefoot College, which promotes rural development through innovative education programs.
- Amitabh Shah {India} - Founder of Yuva Unstoppable, which works for 250,000 underprivileged children mobilizing 100,000 volunteers from 32 cities.
- Muhammad Yunus (Bangladesh) - Founder of microcredit and the Grameen Bank. He was awarded the 2006 Nobel Peace Prize.

- Dr Willie Smits (Borneo, Indonesia) - Founder of the Borneo Orangutan Survival Foundation, Founder and Chairperson of the Masarang Foundation
- Thinlas Chorol (India) - Founder of the Ladadakhi Women's Travel Company, which despite social norms works to bring women into, the otherwise male-dominated Ladakhi tourism industry.
- Nand Kishore Chaudhary (India) - Founder of Jaipur rugs, which promotes rural development through capacity building of rural people in carpet weaving.
- Harish Hande (India) - Founder of Selco India, a solar electric light company in 1995, which over the years has lit up over 120,000 households, to emerge as India's leading solar technology firm.Magsaysay Award 2011.
- Yashveer Singh (India) – Founder of National Social Entrepreneurship Forum, supporting youth-driven social entrepreneurship.
- Sharad Sagar - Founder and CEO, Dexterity Global

Social innovation

From Wikipedia, the free encyclopedia

Social innovation refers to new strategies, concepts, ideas and organizations that meet social needs of all kinds — from working conditions and education to community development and health — and that extend and strengthen civil society.

The term has overlapping meanings. It can be used to refer to social processes of innovation, such as open source methods and techniques. Alternatively it refers to innovations which have a social purpose — like microcredit or distance learning. The concept can also be related to social entrepreneurship and it also overlaps with innovation in public policy and governance. Social innovation can take place within government, the for-profit sector, the nonprofit sector, or in the spaces between them. Research has focused on the types of platforms needed to facilitate such cross-sector collaborative social innovation.

Social Innovation is often an effort of mental creativity which involves fluency and flexibility from a wide range of discipline. The act of social innovation in a sector is mostly connected with diverse disciplines within the society. The social innovation theory of 'connected difference' emphasizes three key dimensions to social innovation. First, they are usually new combination or hybrids of existing elements, rather than wholly new. Two, their practice involve cutting across organizational or disciplinary boundaries and lastly they leave behind compelling new relationships between previously separate individuals and groups. Social innovation is gaining visibility within academia.

Prominent innovators associated with the term include Pakistani Akhter Hameed Khan, Bangladeshi Muhammad Yunus, the founder of Grameen Bank which pioneered the concept of microcredit for supporting innovators in multiple developing countries in Asia, Africa and Latin America, and Stephen Goldsmith, former Indianapolis mayor who engaged the private sector in providing many city services.

History

Social innovation was discussed in the writings of figures such as Peter Drucker and Michael Young in the 1960s. It also appeared in the work of French writers in the 1970s, such as Pierre Rosanvallon, Jacques Fournier, and Jacques Attali. However, the themes and concepts in social innovation existed long before. Benjamin Franklin, for example, talked about small modifications within the social organisation of communities that could help to solve everyday problems. Many radical 19th century reformers like Robert Owen, founder of the cooperative movement, promoted innovation in the social field and all of the great sociologists including Karl Marx, Max Weber and Émile

Durkheim focused attention on broader processes of social change. More detailed theories of social innovation became prominent in the 20th century. Joseph Schumpeter, for example, addressed the process of innovation directly with his theory of creative destruction and his definition of entrepreneurs as people who combined existing elements in new ways to create a new product or service. Beginning in the 1980s, writers on technological change increasingly addressed how social factors affect technology diffusion.

Developments since 2000

Academic research, blogs and websites feature social innovation, along with organizations working on the boundaries of research and practical action. Topics include:

- **Innovation in public services** was pioneered particularly in some Scandinavian and Asian countries. Governments are increasingly recognizing that innovation requires healthcare, schooling and democracy.
- Social entrepreneurship, which is the practice of creating new organizations focusing on non- market activities.
- **Business**, particularly in services.
- **Open source** innovation, in which the intellectual property involved in a product or service, is made freely available.
- **Complex adaptive systems**, which have built-in mechanisms to help them adapt to changing circumstances.
- **Collaborative approaches** which involve stakeholders who are not directly responsible for some activity, such as stockholders and unions collaborating on business issue and business collaborating with government on regulatory issues.
- **Innovation diffusion**
- **Localized influences** that make some localities particularly innovative.

- **Institutional or system entrepreneurship** which focuses on agents who work at a broad system level in order to create the conditions which will allow innovations to have a lasting impact.

Institutional support

The US created an Office for Social Innovation in the White House, which is funding projects that combine public and private resources. Foundations support social innovation. The European Union's innovation strategy was the first well-funded research and development strategy to emphasize social innovation. Public policy makers support social innovation in these different sectors, notably in the UK, Australia, China and Denmark. In 2010, the US government listed 11 investments made by its 'Social Innovation Fund', with public funding more than matched by philanthropic organizations. The fund focuses on partnerships with charities, social enterprises, and business.

Local and Regional development

Literature on social innovation in relation to territorial/ regional development covers innovation in the social economy, i.e. strategies for satisfaction of human needs; and innovation in the sense of transforming and/or sustaining social relations, especially governance relations at the regional and local level. Beginning in the late 1980s, Jean-Louis Laville and Frank Moulaert researched social innovation. In Canada CRISES initiated this type of research. Another, larger project was SINGOCOM a European Commission Framework 5 project, which pioneered so-called "Alternative Models for Local Innovation" (ALMOLIN). These models were further elaborated through community actions covered by KATARSIS and SOCIAL POLIS. More recent works focus on the societal role of the economic life in terms of innovations in social practices and social relations at the local and regional levels. Social Innovation, therefore, is increasingly seen as a process and a strategy to foster human development through solidarity, cooperation, and cultural diversity.

A study by a PhD student from Eastern Michigan University provides preliminary evidence that technological innovation shares causal relation with public health.

The EU funded URBACT programme is designed to help cities to exchange and learn around urban policies. The URBACT methodology can be seen as a social innovation action planning approach. A typical URBACT network would have ten cities working on a specific theme such as active inclusion or regenerating disadvantaged neighborhoods. They examine good practice and then working through a local support group use the results to inform their local action plan.

The Social Innovation Europe initiative, funded by the European Commission's Directorate General for Enterprise and Industry, was set up to map social innovation at a European level, by creating a directory of grass-roots examples of social innovation from across the 27 member states.

Some noted scholars

- Akhtar Hameed Khan
- Jürgen Howaldt & Michael Schwarz
- Jean-Louis Laville
- Frank Moulaert
- Geoff Mulgan
- Michael D. Mumford
- Frances Westley